ISLAM
UNMASKED

endorsements

Now more than ever it is vital for Christians to act responsibly, compassionately and with discernment toward the world's 1.2 billion Muslims. Dr. Henry Malone has invested decades of personal ministry doing just that. His insightful book is an important contribution to understanding the Islamic world and responding with intelligence and spiritual sensitivity to this paramount challenge to the Church.

David Shibley
President, Global Advance
Dallas, Texas

There is an adage that says, "The better we know how our enemy fights, the better we'll be equipped to fight him." How true!

America was taken off guard when the World Trade Center Towers were demolished on September 11th due to the fact that we didn't know how Islam would fight us. *Islam Unmasked* by Dr. Henry Malone lays bare from its beginning how founder Muhammad (670A.D. - 632A.D.) established an evil religion that had as its goal to conquer every nation. How? Through slavery of women, population increase, forced conversions, training young children, discipling in our prisons, murder and bloodshed. Yet America calls Islam, "a peace-loving people."

What does the Koran, their holy book, teach? Some 80 percent of the Arabs can't read, write or speak Arabic. It's up to their caliphates (religious leaders) to interpret the Koran for them. They have no word for salvation. Good works alone are recommended to the 1.2 billion Muslims in the world today.

The average American, saved or unsaved, knows little about Islam. Unless we become knowledgeable of their plans, and learn how to bring salvation to them through Jesus, we'll lose the battle. We dare not allow Islam to tranquilize us!

That's why I recommend so highly you read *Islam Unmasked* and share it with others.

> **Freda Lindsey**
> *Co-Founder, Christ for the Nations*
> *Dallas, Texas*

Most Christians have many questions and very few answers when it comes to Islam because we have simply not been informed. This work by Dr. Henry Malone is the best I've ever read on this subject. I believe it gives the answers we have all looked for such as, why does our President tolerate this evil? Who is Allah? And how peaceful is this religion? As far as I am concerned, it is a must have book.

> **Olen Griffing**
> *Founding Pastor, Shady Grove Church*
> *Grand Prairie, Texas*

In a time of much media disinformation, filtered through unholy agendas, this book is a welcome relief. While God loves those of the Islam faith, He does not love the Islam faith itself. In *Islam Unmasked*, Henry Malone reveals the clear and present danger that Islam presents not only to the Body of Christ, but also to the world. Wise men will head the warning contained herein.

John Paul Jackson
Founder and Chairman, Streams Ministries International
North Sutton, New Hampshire

ISLAM UNMASKED

DR. HENRY MALONE

First printing 2002

Requests for information should be addressed to:
Vision Life Publications, P.O. Box 153691, Irving, TX 75015
Office: (972) 251-7170 Fax: (972) 254-1510
Email: vlm@visionlife.org Web site: www.visionlife.org

Unless otherwise noted, all Scripture quotations are taken
from the *King James Version* and from *The Holy Bible, New
King James Version*. Copyright 1979, 1980, 1982 Thomas
Nelson, Inc.

ISBN 097170651-4
Designed by Ed Tuttle
Printed in the United States of America

To THE 1.2 BILLION MUSLIMS
around the world who are captives to the deception and
bondage of Islam: May the love of God so touch the
hearts of these men, women and children that they are
transformed forever. My prayer is that they experience
the love, peace and freedom that comes from being in
relationship with Jesus as Savior and Lord.

To THE EVANGELISTS AND MISSIONARIES
in the Islamic countries of the world who unselfishly
give of their lives: My prayer is that God would protect,
strengthen and empower them with His life-changing
anointing. May their labor in His fields bring forth a
mighty harvest for the kingdom of God.

contents

Islam has had a face unknown to the majority of the people here in the West. After September 11, the true face and reality of the Islamic faith is being uncovered to us by various people who are aware of the deceitfulness of this seventh century religion.

Dr. Henry Malone has labored as a missionary among the Muslim people for many years. His understanding of the Islamic faith is not attained by reading some history books, but rather by dealing with the Muslim people for many years. In this book, Dr. Malone helps us to understand the true nature of Islam. Is Islam peaceful, as we have been told? Is the God of Islam the Jehovah of the Bible? Is Mohammad sent by God? Is the Koran a holy book? These are some of the unanswered questions that Dr. Malone will answer for us in his book, *Islam Unmasked.*

I was born and raised a radical Shiite Muslim. I have known the reality of the nature of Islam by practicing every law of it. I would like to commend Dr. Malone for writing this wonderful book and opening our eyes to the challenge that is set before us. There are 1.2 billion Muslims who are bound by the forces of a dark and a demonic religion. Let us see the truth and let us proclaim freedom for the captives of Islam.

For His Glory,
Pastor Reza F. Safa
Harvest Church
Tulsa, Oklahoma

acknowledgements

I would like to express my deepest appreciation for the following people who have contributed to making this book a reality:

- ➤ My wife, Tina, who oversees all the general operations of the ministry.

- ➤ Donna Hilton who edited and proofed the manuscript.

- ➤ Susan Martin who helped with research.

- ➤ Edward Tuttle who designed the cover and layout.

- ➤ Pastor Reza Safa who graciously gave of his time to read the manuscript, give input and write the foreword.

- ➤ George Arneson who gave valuable input from his research.

Islam on the World Stage
Looking Behind the Mask

He was born in the year A.D. 570 in a city in Arabia. His father died at his birth. His mother shortly afterward before his sixth birthday.

He was placed into the care of his grandfather who soon died. His uncle became his next guardian and introduced him to a powerful tribe. For the moment death had left him. But it would revisit him later in life and taunt him to commit suicide. After his death, his followers would be willing to die in his honor and kill others in his name.

America would learn his tenets of death on September 11, 2001, when his followers would take off their mask of peace and reveal their true face—one of hatred, violence and death. They would take their sword from its sheath, unleash their bloodthirsty spirit and send four planes into New York, Pennsylvania and Washington, D.C. Within moments they would attempt to leave a lasting mark of terror and deception across the United States.

While America tried to cope with the worst terrorist strike in its history, Osama bin Laden's comrades in arms would celebrate the hitting of their targets.

Following the horror of the attacks, many have been confused and deceived about Islam. People everywhere have heard the news media call those who perpetrated the act of war against America fanatics and not true believers of Allah.

Even the President has called the religion one of "peace" and has encouraged all Americans to recognize the right of everyone to worship their "own god." And those who have raised their voices to speak of the hidden agenda behind Islam have been accused of not being tolerant and faced recrimination.

> I want to expose the deception by the enemy of all of our souls, who has fostered lies and kept those who practice Islam from seeing the truth.

What is the truth? What is the history of Muhammad and Islam? What are its doctrines? Who is Allah? Is Islam really a peaceful religion? What is Paradise and who can go there? How do Moslems view women? How do Christians break down the barriers and find common ground?

Throughout the pages of this book I will examine and answer all of these questions.

As I do, I want you, the reader, to hear my heart. It is not my intention to create an adversarial atmosphere or an attitude of hatred toward Muslims. I have a deep love for all Muslims.

Instead I want to expose the deception by the enemy of all of our souls, who has fostered lies and kept those who practice Islam from seeing the truth regarding its false foundations and demonic strongholds.

It is my prayer that this book will educate Christians all across this nation and around the world. It is my hope that the seducing spirits behind Islam will be exposed and the barriers broken down between Muslims and Christians.

It is my heart's deepest desire that Christians lead many Muslims into a life-changing experience with Jesus Christ through the truth of the Word of God, the power of the Holy Spirit, and the love of God. Now let's take the mask off Islam.

one

The Propaganda War
The Real Story

We are in a war.

It is a battle for the souls inhabiting planet earth. And Satan, the enemy of mankind, has fostered his own point of view and dropped into the heart of every person his own form of misinformation.

Throughout the ages he has waged a propaganda war. Nowhere has this war been more effective than in the arena of religion. Lucifer, the angel of light, the deceiver, made it his mission to lie regarding the One true God and His Son, Jesus Christ.

Part of his relentless campaign has been to encourage men and women everywhere to create and serve a "god" of their own choosing and often of their own making.

Back to the Garden

Satan started in the Garden of Eden when he convinced Eve that the God she thought she knew was keeping her from being like Him. He persuaded her to believe that she could be her "own god." But, in truth, God had already made her exactly like Him (Genesis 1:26).

Eve took from the tree of good and evil and partook of the self-rule and independence that would separate her from God. The spirit of divination entered her life. The serpent's false light blinded her from the truth and sowed the seeds of rebellion and independence in her heart. She was deceived.

Her husband, Adam, was not deceived. He saw behind the mixture of truth and error, but he was taken in by the fake illumination. His desire for Eve, without the covering of God's glory, caused him to choose disobedience rather than obedience.

Adam took the fruit, ate it and sowed the seeds of whoredom and idolatry into his heart. He would lose the close communion he shared with God and fall perilously into the deception of his new master—Satan. His relationships with God and his wife would never be the same.

A Growing Deception

The serpent of old had won the propaganda war. He had pushed Eve, Adam and those who would come after them to embrace deception, lust and the worship of other gods. And he continued to win his war with their son Cain.

When Cain chose to set his own parameters for worship, he practiced the idolatry of his father and mother. And when he refused to set aside his anger toward his brother, he allowed Satan to sow the seeds of jealousy, anger, wrath, rage and murder into his heart.

Then the bloodline of Cain continued to walk in murder and death. So along with their spirits of divination, whoredom and idolatry, they added the spirit of antichrist.

When Nimrod, the son of Cush, the grandson of Ham, the great-grandson of Noah and the great-great-grandson of Lamech, built the Tower of Babel, he attempted to ascend and assume a lofty, exalted place. He wanted to take over God's position, thus creating another way to God.

All false religions have built on those same foundations of the spirits of divination, whoredom, idolatry and antichrist. Nimrod grew his own tree of good and evil and produced his own fruit of deception.

Building False Foundations

Satan continues to use this same line of deception today. He deceives many into believing there are many paths to God, and builds false foundations for other religions by leading people away from the one light and one truth. He encourages men and women to take fruit from his tree of deception.

Jesus warned of the lure and deception of false teaching and false prophets in Matthew 7:15-20. There he outlined a litmus test for determining truth from deception and light from darkness: "Beware of false prophets, who come to you in sheep's clothing, but inwardly they are ravenous wolves. You will know them by their fruits. Do men gather grapes from thornbushes or figs from thistles?

> **Satan deceives many into believing there are many paths to God, leading people away from the one light and truth.**

Even so, every good tree bears good fruit, but a bad tree bears bad fruit. A good tree cannot bear bad fruit, nor can a bad tree bear good fruit. Every tree that does not bear good fruit is cut down and thrown into the fire. Therefore by their fruits you will know them."

Why can many not see the fruit of Islam? Why are so many deceived? Why do some believe the error of Islam's teachings?

A Question of Authority

During the last few months, the news media have told millions around the world that only the fanatical fringe perpetuates the violence of Islam. Why do they not see the error in Islam's teachings?

Even President George W. Bush has often spoken and declared Islam to be a religion of peace. Why doesn't he see the lie? After all, he's a Christian. Doesn't he know that we don't serve the same God?

How is this possible?

The answer to that question lies not in the deception behind Islam, but in the authority that God has delegated to different spiritual realms, governments and individuals.

The news media do not have spiritual authority. The Fox Network, MSNBC and CBS are not the messengers of God. They are news organizations chartered by the FCC to present a fair and balanced picture of events and people around the world.

God *has* given authority in three places—the home, the government and the Church. He created them to be separate authorities, independent of each other yet interdependent.

The government is to provide an atmosphere of peace, justice and equality for its citizens. The family is to operate as a place of love, protection and provision for its members. And the Church is to be the living picture of God's love and glory in the earth.

> God has given authority in the home, the government and the Church, creating them to be independent of each other yet interdependent.

Satan's interference, and man's sin, has left God's original plans for all three realms of authority twisted and separated from their true spiritual purposes. If we could only see God's true operation of these authorities we would understand how interconnected they really are.

America is not a theocracy where everyone must serve God and Him only. The president, as commander in chief of the United States of America, is not a priest, but a judicial head of state, exercising his God-given authority. He is not placed as a ruler to judge the beliefs of other religions. God has positioned him to rule.

The President's responsibility is to provide freedom and peace for all Americans so that they might live as Paul says in Romans 12:18, "...peaceably with all men." When President Bush speaks he is not endorsing a religion, but advocating freedom to worship for all Americans.

On September 17, 2001, he said, "America counts millions of Muslims amongst our citizens, and Muslims make an incredibly valuable contribution to our country. Muslims are doctors, lawyers, law professors, members of the military, entrepreneurs, shopkeepers, moms and dads. And they need to be treated with respect. In our anger and emotion, our fellow Americans must treat each other with respect."

Our President is doing the right thing. He is promoting peace and discouraging strife, division and violence. He is sowing seeds of brotherly love among those of different races and religions. He is fulfilling that which he was called to do.

> For rulers are not a terror to good works, but to evil. Do you want to be unafraid of the authority? Do what is good, and you will have praise from the same. For he is God's minister to you for good. But if you do evil, be afraid; for he does not bear the sword in vain; for he is God's minister, an avenger to execute wrath on him who practices evil (Romans 13:3-4).

Authorities at Odds?

When Franklin Graham, the son of the Rev. Billy Graham, made his statement against Islam on November 16, the White House distanced itself from his remarks. Graham said, speaking of Islam, "I don't believe this is a wonderful, peaceful religion....When you read the Quran, it instructs the killing of the infidel, for those that are non-Muslim....It wasn't Methodists flying into those buildings, it wasn't Lutherans, it was an attack on this country by people of the Islamic faith."

Are Mr. Graham and President Bush at odds?

Not really. They are merely exercising their different roles and responsibilities within the realm of their authority.

Mr. Graham was responding as a religious cleric in his role as a priest of the Church. The President was responding in his role as a head of state.

The President continues to be dedicated to avoiding a face-off in the natural and spiritual arena. He has no interest in perpetuating a Jihad holy war of "death to the infidels." The exercise of his authority in the judicial realm of government is not at cross purposes to the authority of the priestly realm of the Church.

The Church's Authority

The Church has been given authority by God to expose the truth from the lie, and light from darkness. We have been called to preach the gospel of the good news of Jesus Christ and lead people away from the deception of Satan's propaganda, no matter what kind it is.

We have been chartered with exposing the seducing spirits and doctrines of demons that lead people everywhere from the truth. We have been given the position and privilege of leading people into a life-changing relationship with the only Son of God. We have been given the Word of God to teach the truth, the power of the Holy Spirit to minister hope, healing, and deliverance, and the love of God to bring reconciliation and build relationships between people.

Jesus commanded, "Go into all the world and preach the gospel to every creature. He who believes and is baptized will be saved; but he who does not believe will be condemned. And these signs will follow those who believe: In My name they will cast out demons; they will speak with new tongues; they will take up serpents; and if they drink anything deadly, it will by no means hurt them; they will lay hands on the sick, and they will recover" (Mark 16:15-18). God has given us the authority to go to all the nations of the world in His Name.

Authority has also been delegated to the realm of the personal. God has given us authority in our individual lives and homes. As individuals we must decide whether we will choose to serve God or Satan. We must practice the truth or be pulled into deception. We must walk in light or take the path toward darkness.

We can exchange the truth for a lie and be transformed by the power of God's Word that translates us from darkness into the light. What the government cannot legislate and the Church cannot impose, we can choose to exercise within the walls of our own households, both as individuals and as a family unit.

Our neighbors, friends and family should see the difference in our lives. They should see the evidence of the power of God operating every day.

Are we speaking what we believe, or are we living it? All of us have the opportunity to be the living evidence of God's Word. We can all be the "living Word of God" to those around us.

The Church has been given authority by God to expose the truth from the lie, and light from darkness.

Possibly you have believed the enemy's propaganda. You might have already tuned in to hear his point of view. Maybe you've even accepted the false teaching that all roads really do "lead to Rome." You might have looked at Islam and seen the deceptive "friendly mask" instead of its demonic face.

If you have made the decision to be tolerant of the false light, open your eyes to see the truth of what God is saying about Islam. Look at the tree and the fruit. Decide to no longer be deceived by the seducing spirits of divination, whoredom, idolatry and antichrist, and the wolves that come in sheep's clothing.

Remember a bad tree cannot bear good fruit. Look at the tree. Examine the fruit. Then search for the roots. The roots determine the fruit.

two

The Issue of Authority

Power in Three Realms

Good is not the author of chaos. He is a God of order, with a specifically defined system of authority and power, and the rules for their operation.

The question surrounding the issue of authority is not whether or not it exists, but what form it takes. God has built into the earth rules of authority between husbands and wives, parents and children, churches and their people, governments and their people, and Jesus over the Church.

The Ultimate Authority

The word "authority" comes from the Greek word exousia or the "freedom of action." It is this right, ability and freedom of action that sets up God's power system in three realms.

God has ultimate authority. He declares of Himself in Isaiah 46:9-11, "Remember the former things of old, For I am God, and there is no other; I am God, and there is none like Me, Declaring the end from the beginning, And from ancient times things that are not yet done, Saying, 'My counsel shall stand, And I will do all My pleasure,' Calling a bird of prey from the east, The man who executes My counsel, from a far country. Indeed I have spoken it; I will also bring it to pass. I have purposed it; I will also do it."

There is no question that God with His authority and power determines history and controls events. Yet He has chosen to share His power with His creation—man. He has given man, both male and female, authority in the earth as individuals, within the family, the government and the Church.

The Family

Every individual believer has authority. For the purposes of this book, I will focus on the delegated authority in the realms of the family, the government and the Church. These three most directly affect society and carry the broadest influence in the earth.

In the family, God has delegated His power to the husband and father, the wife and mother, and the children. He has set in place a rule of order that brings peace, protection and power into the home. No person within the family structure is more important or significant than the other, but all work together.

The father is no more important than any of his children, and the wife is not less significant than her husband. Their different roles and authority bring strength, not weakness, into the household.

Husband and Father

The father and husband is charged to love, serve and give himself to his wife and family as Jesus gave Himself to the Church. He is to use the privilege of his God-given authority with love, care and respect. He is to relate to his wife and family like Jesus does to His Church.

Charles Kraft, in his book *I Give You Authority,* puts it this way: "It is an authority first to love, then to care for; to respect, to sacrifice for and to protect our wives as more vulnerable than we are. Ours is an authority to relate to our wives as Christ relates to His Church.

"Indeed, we are commanded to treat them as Christ treats the Church, giving our lives for them as Jesus gave His life for His Church. This is an incredible mandate. It is authority involving far more responsibility than privilege—an authority that challenges our tendency to see authority as more a matter of rights than of duties. One important responsibility of a husband is to protect his wife and family."

> **The father and husband is to use the privilege of his God-given authority with love, care and respect, relating to his wife and family like Jesus does to His Church.**

The husband and father becomes the spiritual gatekeeper for the family. Kraft says, "This means that whatever spiritual influences enter the family come as a result of the exercise of his authority to consciously or unconsciously give or withhold his permission. The father is in the position either to allow negative or to invite positive spiritual influences into his family."

The husband and father is the head of the household and responsible to keep his family free from Satan and his demonic forces that would try to gain control over his home, land, property and possessions.

Wife and Mother

The wife and mother is to submit to her husband with love and respect as the Church submits to the authority of Jesus. Even though her authority is second to that of her husband in the family structure, she carries power in her relationship with him and their children. She has parental authority and is often the one to exercise it with their children.

Her actions and prayers frequently prevent satanic interference and attacks, as well as restrict the influence of the demonic within the household. When the husband is an unbeliever, the wife carries even more power in the realm of the spirit to cancel demonic assignments, exercise parental authority and represent the light of God to her husband and children.

Children

God has also established rules of authority for children within a household. While they are to submit to their parents' authority, they have the right to exercise their God-given authority over possessions and their own living space.

Children should be protected through the exercise of their parents' authority. They should be able to enjoy safety, peace and the presence of God as they grow and later experience their own relationship with Jesus.

The Fracturing of Households

The family structure has greatly changed over the past decades. As we continue into the first years of the millennium, more and more men, women and children are dealing with the fracturing of their households. Even within the Christian community, divorce is a common occurrence.

God has not left single-parent families without authority. Single mothers and fathers carry the same authority as two-parent families. They have authority and power and provide the same covering for their children.

Many have chosen to bolster their own authority by seeking an additional man—a pastor, surrogate father, grandfather or spiritual leader—to be another covering and authority for their household. Whatever their choice, single parents are not without the presence, protection and power of God.

The Government

When authority is exercised in the natural realm, it is spiritual authority, whether it occurs in the family, the government or the Church. God chooses whom He gives His power to.

One realm He has delegated His authority to is kings, rulers and governments. Paul, in his letter to the Church at Rome, clearly established God's order of authority placed into the hands of human governments.

In Chapter 13 of the book of Romans, Paul says, "Let every soul be subject to the governing authorities. For there is no authority except from God, and the authorities that exist are appointed by God. Therefore whoever resists the authority resists the ordinance of God, and those who resist will bring judgment on themselves" (Romans 13:1-2).

God leaves little question as to who is responsible for placing authority into the hands of men, and the consequences that come to those who refuse to honor them.

An Atmosphere of Peace

God has put governments in place to deal with the natural, judicial and governmental realm, not the spiritual realm. Governments are not given authority over individuals, except in the arena of law and government. They are not put in charge over families and their households.

> Many single parents have bolstered their authority by seeking a pastor, surrogate father, grandfather or spiritual leader to be another covering and authority for their household.

Governments have not been given authority in the realm of the spirit, so they are not responsible over the Church. Romans 13:3-4 specifically states their purpose: "For rulers are not a terror to good works, but to evil. Do you want to be unafraid of the authority? Do what is good, and you will have praise from the same. For he is God's minister to you for good. But if you do evil, be afraid; for he does not bear the sword in vain; for he is God's minister, an avenger to execute wrath on him who practices evil."

Governments are to provide an atmosphere of peace, not to mandate religions or spiritual activities.

Much misunderstanding has arisen during the days following the

September 11 attacks regarding the line between religion and the government. While George W. Bush is a born-again Christian, it is not his responsibility to judge the religion of Islam in his position as president of the United States. He is responsible instead to assure a peaceful atmosphere where Muslims can worship Allah, Christians can exalt Jesus Christ and others can pursue their religious beliefs.

When Muslim, Jewish and Christian clergy participated in the September 14 service in the National Cathedral in Washington, D.C., the Rev. Billy Graham's keynote message was unquestionably and appropriately Christian. The service did not attempt to cast a critical or discerning eye on any of the representative religions, but, instead, to provide a forum for all Americans to express their personal beliefs.

Once again, even in this most tragic of times, the president was establishing an atmosphere of peace. We are blessed to have this freedom to worship in peace.

The Responsibility of Power

Even when government rule is harsh, the Word of God is clear. God has ordained rulers and governments and has commanded believers to recognize their authority. First Peter 2:18 says, "Servants, be submissive to your masters with all fear, not only to the good and gentle, but also to the harsh."

Often, because of sin, society and government have had to limit freedoms and use coercive powers to enforce the laws of the land. As believers we are to obey, knowing that God will judge those He has placed in authority.

> God never delegated authority to man to be used to humiliate, control, overpower or dominate others. He set it up to bring freedom and protection.

But rulers and governments must be careful to not take their position and power lightly. Their obedience or disobedience to God affects all they rule over. Their actions are not exempt, and the effects not without long-term ramifications.

Authority is a privilege that must be exercised in love and wisdom. Within any structure ordained by God, all those in authority must remember that God has set His system of order in place to create an atmosphere of love, peace, protection and His presence. God never delegated authority to man to be used to humiliate, control, overpower or dominate others. He set it up to bring freedom and protection.

The Church

Jesus did not leave His Church without power and authority when He ascended into Heaven to sit at His Father's right hand. Before Jesus released His commission to His followers, He said, "I have been given all authority in heaven and on earth" (Matthew 28:18, *Today's English Version*).

He wanted those who believed in Him to know that the keys of death, hell and the grave had been taken from Satan and his demonic forces. And now, the keys of the kingdom of God were passing into their hands.

Before they went out into the world and changed it forever with the good news of the gospel, He wanted them to know beyond the shadow of a doubt that they had authority. They had His authority and it was the power and authority to affect the earth. Then He said, "Go, then, to all peoples everywhere and make them my disciples: baptize them in the name of the Father, the Son, and the Holy Spirit, and teach them to obey everything I have commanded you..." (verses 19-20, *Today's English Version*).

The Gospel of Mark, Chapter 16 records a slightly different version. It says in verses 15-18, "Go into all the world and preach the gospel to every creature. He who believes and is baptized will be saved; but he who does not believe will be condemned. And these signs will follow those who believe: In My name they will cast out demons; they will speak with new tongues; they will take up serpents; and if they drink anything deadly, it will by no means hurt them; they will lay hands on the sick, and they will recover."

His power released in believers is not without signs. It is not without astounding and lasting evidence of His presence. The Church is the visible evidence of Jesus in the earth. He intended that we make a lasting impact in the world around us and be a living witness of the change He has made in our lives.

When the Church refuses to accept and exercise its God-given authority, Satan takes the upper hand and moves in to influence and change the world. In doing so he is taking our position in the earth.

Submitting to Authority

The Church must see and understand what Satan is trying to do in the hearts of men and women throughout the earth. God is not interested in us being "politically correct." C. Peter Wagner puts it this way in his *Global Prayer News:* "Worship of Allah, no matter how sincere or pure-hearted, will not get a person to Heaven any more than worship of Inti or Amaterasu Omikami or Zeus or Guadalupe or Maximon or Baal or Quetzalcoatl or Kali or whatever one's created demonic spirit of choice might be."

Satan has successfully pulled the wool over the eyes of the world as they walk in darkness. He also is determined to keep the Church from unmasking the lies of Islam.

Before we can make a lasting impact in the earth, we must be subject to God's authority and the authority of those He has placed throughout the Body of Christ.

The Leadership of the Church

In order to exercise our authority we must first be willing to submit *to* authority. And the Church, for the most part, has been unwilling to be obedient. They have refused to accept His authority and so have chosen rebellion.

Rebellion is nothing more than service to Satan. In fact, the Word of God calls it the sin of witchcraft.

Every believer is either submitted to God's authority, or in rebellion and serving Satan. There is no middle ground. Sadly though it is our rebellion that will keep the world around us from knowing God.

Help Not Harm

Not only have believers refused to submit to God's authority, they have ignored His delegated authority—Church leadership. Pastors, elders and deacons were placed in authority not to control, manipulate or dominate, but to serve as spiritual gatekeepers and shepherds of the flock. They were meant to teach, encourage, admonish and protect.

The five-fold ministry of apostles, prophets, evangelists, pastors and teachers were designed by God to equip the Church and help all believers to "...grow up in all things into Him who is the head—Christ—from whom the whole body, joined and knit together by what every joint supplies, according to the effective working by which every part does its share, causes growth of the body for the edifying of itself in love" (Ephesians 4:15-16).

> **Every believer is either submitted to God's authority, or in rebellion and serving Satan. There is no middle ground.**

Just as with the family and government, God intended for the Church to benefit people, not harm them. But Satan has used what God intended for good. He has twisted the purposes of these authorities and has made it difficult, if not impossible, for many people to trust those over them—even those within the Church.

The Church, unified in love and functioning as many different parts of the whole, is still God's picture of Himself to the world. When we as believers will submit to God's authority, find our place in the Body of Christ—His Church—and function in unity and love, then the world will see Jesus.

Then, when they see Him, they will never be the same again. God's commission to His Church will be fulfilled, and signs, wonders and miracles will appear around the world as everyday evidence of His power and presence in the earth.

three

The History of Islam
A Bloody Thread

Imagine the vast deserts that fill the land between the Red Sea and the Indian Ocean. Picture fertile valleys and coastal cities. Mix in the culture of the sixth century with its many tribes. Factor in the importance of business to the city of Mecca and you have the future birthplace of a religion.

It was there along the main trade route between the East and West that Islam was born. There in the city making its wealth through the sale of hundreds of idols the new religion took hold. And the pagan roots of the religion were undeniable.

The people of Arabia worshiped many different deities. Mecca was a shrine city where the Ka'aba was located.

The Ka'aba or house of Allah was filled with idols and images of other gods and goddesses. People on their pilgrimage to the city would walk around the cubical building seven times, touching and kissing the huge black stone that was within. The meteorite had pagan roots and

19

was of great religious significance to its worshipers.

One of those who worshiped at the base of the stone was Abdullah.

Muhammad—Slave of Allah

Muhammad's father, Abdullah (slave of Allah) belonged to the Hashim clan—a subgrouping of the dominant tribe of the area called Quarish. Abdullah had only been married to Aminah for six months when he joined a caravan heading for Syria.

He left his wife, tearful and pregnant, hoping to make his fortune. Instead he would catch a fever and die. His wife would be left alone to give birth to her child.

While her husband was still alive and on his journey, Aminah's handmaiden had a dream. She told her mistress that her unborn child would be a son and that she should name him Muhammad. The name, never before used by this tribe, meant "high praised."

When the child was born, the news of his father's death had already reached his wife. His grandfather, Abdel Muttalib, tried to comfort the grieving widow. He said that his newly born grandson would be a little Abdullah, slave to Allah.

It was customary at the time for parents that lived in the city to send their young children to the country to be cared for by foster mothers. These caretakers would go door to door offering their services. They did not, however, knock on the door of Aminah. Instead her father-in-law found a foster mother and Muhammad was sent off to be raised by the tribe of Sa'ad.

After he left for the country, a plague hit Mecca. Muhammad stayed in the country longer than usual to avoid death, but was returned to his natural mother before he turned 6.

Shortly after his return home, Aminah took her son and servant, Barakah, to visit relatives in Yathrib. They stopped at her husband's grave and then made the 10-day trip northward.

Once in Yathrib they enjoyed their time with relatives. On the return trip home, Aminah became sick with a fever and died. But before her death, she made Barakah promise to take care of her son. For the next two years Barakah and Muhammad would live with Abdel Muttalib until his death.

After the grandfather's death, Barakah took Muhammad to the house of his uncle, Abu Talib. He would spend the rest of his early years there. He was only 10, but had already been orphaned three times.

Throughout his youth and teenage years he tended his uncle's sheep. He had little time for himself. And unlike others his age he avoided fighting, drinking and prostitutes. Instead he developed a reputation for honesty and integrity.

Muhammad became restless. He began searching for the meaning and mystery of life.

Muhammad's uncle arranged his marriage to a wealthy widow named Khadija. When they married, Muhammad was 25 and his wife was 40. They later would have four daughters and two sons. His sons would both die in infancy.

Muhammad became restless. He began searching for the meaning and mystery of life.

One day as he was sitting in a cave thinking about the real meaning behind all of life, a light appeared and a voice, he described as frightening and compelling, commanded him to read.

But Muhammad couldn't read. He was illiterate.

He felt as if his breath was being taken away.

Again the voice commanded him to read. He protested reminding this voice that he couldn't read. And the command was given a third and final time.

Fearful that he couldn't handle the pain any longer he responded, "What should I read?"

The Quran, Sura 96:1-5 gives the answer: "Read in the Name of your Lord Who created humans from a clinging. Read for your Lord is the Most Generous. He taught people by the pen what they didn't know before." Another version of the same passage reads, "Recite, in the name of the Lord who has created, created man from the clots of blood.

Recite, seeing that the Lord is the most generous, who has taught by the pen, taught man what he did not know."

He ran from the cave to his home. He was scared, but his wife, Khadija, comforted him. She told him that the voice he heard was God.

Muhammad wasn't sure.

Messenger of God?

Throughout the next 23 years Muhammad said that the one who had come to him wasn't God at all but, instead, was Gabriel, a messenger of God. According to this self-proclaimed prophet, the archangel of God brought these revelations.

Had Muhammad encountered God or an angel? Was his messenger the same spirit that spoke to Nimrod, Joseph Smith and many others who founded false religions?

What was behind these visions of light? And why after these visitations did he consider taking his own life? Why had his search for truth caused him such despair?

Reza F. Safa, in his book *Inside Islam–Exposing and Reaching the World of Islam*, sheds more light on Muhammad's early spiritual experiences:

"For some months, during which time no more revelations came to Muhammad, he was deeply depressed and even considered suicide. After two years other revelations began

> **When a revelation came to Muhammed, he would fall to the ground and foam at the mouth.**

to come to Muhammad in various forms. Sometimes he saw an angel; sometimes he only heard a voice, and sometimes a message came in a dream. When a revelation came to him, he would fall to the ground and foam at the mouth."

As a minister of the gospel for 40 years, I have never seen God speak to a man through a manifestation of foaming at the mouth. I have, however, over the past 15 years in deliverance ministry, seen many a demon reveal its presence in that same way.

Channel of Revelations

He couldn't write, so Muhammad's channeled revelations were dictated by others who wrote them down and put them in a volume known as the Quran. The Quran is made up of 114 chapters or Suras, and more than 6,600 verses called ayats that cover a wide range of subjects.

Before long Muhammad was preaching that there was no God but Allah. He regarded himself as Allah's prophet and mouthpiece. He called on the people to repent, stop worshiping other gods and turn to Allah alone.

Gathering Followers

Muhammad's first converts were members of his own family including his wife, their adopted son, Zaid, and a cousin, Ali. Soon 100 more people had joined the cause, most of whom were of humble origins.

Persecution shortly followed as the business leaders attacked Muhammad for his stance against the gods of Ka'aba. Change was coming for Muhammad.

By the year 620, his wife and uncle had died. It wasn't long after his wife's death that he married a young widow who was one of his followers. At the same time, he also married the 7-year-old daughter of a close friend.

His religion promoted purity of heart and good moral conduct, but his prophetic revelations held him to a different standard. The Quran, Sura 33:50 says, "O prophet! We have made lawful to thee thy wives to whom thou hast paid their dowers; and those whom thy right hand possesses out of the prisoners of war whom God, has assigned to thee; and daughters of thy paternal uncles and aunts, and daughters of thy maternal uncles and aunts who migrated with thee; and any believing woman who dedicates her soul to the prophet if the prophet wishes to wed her;—this only for thee, and not for believers; we know what we have appointed for them as to their wives and the captives whom their right hand possess;—in order that there should be no difficulty for thee. And God is oft-forgiving, most merciful."

Wives and Mistresses

Muhammad's prophetic revelations had given him permission to take 14 wives and the special privilege to have as many mistresses as he desired. His passion for women was insatiable. He even took the only wife of his adopted son, Zaid, saying to him, "Praise belongeth unto Allah who turneth the hearts of men as he willeth."

Zaid got the prophet's message and divorced his wife, Zainab.

In order to cover his detestable act he received a revelation timed just before the divorce was finalized. The Quran, Sura 33:37, says, "Behold! Thou didst say to one who had received the grace of God and thy Favor; 'retain thou thy wife, and fear God.' But thou didst fear in thy heart that which God was about to make manifest: thou didst fear the people, but it is more fitting that thou should fear God. Then when Zaid had dissolved with her, with the necessary, we joined her in marriage to thee: in order that in there may be no difficulty to the believers in marriage with the wives of their adopted sons, when the later have dissolved with the necessary with them. And God's command must be fulfilled."

So much for Muhammad's purity of heart and his commitment to a moral lifestyle.

Trouble on the Horizon

Indiscretions aside, without the protection and encouragement of his wife and the influence of his uncle, Muhammad wasn't making much progress. He moved from Mecca to Yathrib, a city 250 miles north. It would later be known as Medina, or the city of the prophet.

The date was September 24, 622. Islam was born. Financial difficulties, division, violence and broken treaties were on the horizon, foreshadowing the dark face of this new religion.

Muhammad had been in Medina for only two years when things became financially difficult for him and many of his followers. It was during this period that he received a revelation: "O Prophet, strive hard against unbelievers and be firm against them" (Quran 9:73).

The seeds of hatred and vengeance for the "infidels" and all who were opposed to Islam had already been sown.

Thinking that he had divine approval, Muhammad soon began to raid the caravans of his enemies. The taking of smaller caravans led to raids on larger ones until finally he and his 350 armed men attacked a caravan at Badr. They defeated an army of 1,000 and collected their spoils. He divided the merchandise with his men and took a fifth of all that had been taken for himself.

His victory brought him confidence that Allah was with him. But even greater problems were on the way.

> The seeds of hatred and vengeance for the "infidels" and all who were opposed to Islam had already been sown.

Muhammad had always been at odds with the Jewish community of the city. He claimed to be a prophet. The Jews knew he wasn't their Messiah.

The division of the city became clear when several of Muhammad's followers assassinated a group of Jews. And they continued their attacks on the Jewish tribes of the area. They massacred a thousand men in one battle, sold the women and children into slavery and divided their property among the soldiers.

In 628, with the death and destruction mounting, the Quraish in Mecca sought to forge a treaty with Muhammad and his followers. They agreed to keep the peace and cease fighting for the next 10 years.

Within two short years, Muhammad had broken the treaty. He attacked Mecca with his army of 10,000 and took control of the city. He destroyed the idols of the Ka'aba and executed many of the city's people.

He became a force to be reckoned with and the political and religious leader of Arabia. Mecca now belonged to him. It was conversion to Islam or death.

In only 10 more years—in 632—Muhammad would be dead. His followers would wage a struggle for power and divide their religion into two factions—the Shia, or Shiites, and the Sunnites.

Civil War in the Making

The history of Islam had only started. At the time of Muhammad's death, Islam was the major power across the Arabian Peninsula.

Muhammad's first caliph, Abu Baker, united the tribes under Islamic rule. Omar, the second caliph, collapsed both the Persian and Byzantine empires and brought Islam to the regions of what today we call Iraq, Iran and Central Asia. He and his armies conquered all of Asia and the former Roman empire except the area that we would refer to today as Turkey. Then they took control of Syria and Damascus.

His caliphs expanded the reach of Islam through Egypt, across North Africa and into much of Europe including Spain. Their relentless expansion was finally stopped at the Battle of Tours in France. In the span

> By the later half of the 20th century, the same forces that transformed Iran, Sudan and Afghanistan were waiting to change the world.

of 100 years, Islam had built an empire. Despite their victories a civil war was brewing which, in many ways, still rages today.

For a little over a hundred years, the killing and hatred between groups of Muslims continued. By the 10th century all of the caliphs had lost their power and the empire they had worked so hard to build was falling apart.

In 1258, Baghdad fell to the Mongolian army. Less than 300 years later, in the 15th century, Islam had recovered from its losses and begun to expand their territory. It emerged and flourished as the Ottoman empire, expanding into the Balkan Peninsula, moving into Hungary and along Asia Minor, Armenia and Egypt. And it finally touched the north coast of Africa.

While Islam stopped short of Vienna, it managed to infiltrate both Iraq and Arabia and regain ground. Islam even found its way into areas where Christianity had been the majority religion.

In the 16th century, mandatory conversion was commonplace and many Christians who were slaves to Muslim masters converted. Others conformed to Islam to escape the persecution of Orthodox and Catholic Christians. Frequently, sons of Christian fathers were torn from their families, sent to Muslim homes and enrolled in Islamic armies. Churches were changed to mosques overnight.

European colonization came in the 18th and 19th centuries and wiped out the Islamic stronghold, leaving few states behind. Once again, to everyone's surprise, Islam rebounded after World War II. Most of the areas once colonized in the early 18th century received their independence and became part of the global network—the United Nations.

By the 20th century, Islam had a different face, a newfound power and a lasting identity—oil.

By the later half of the 20th century, Islamic fundamentalism had taken hold. A dozen countries threatened to embrace Islam and turn their governments into theocracies. The same forces that had transformed Iran, Sudan and Afghanistan were waiting to change the world. Those changes would bring trademarks of Islam to the forefront—massive terrorism, intolerance, dominion and eventual world impacting revolution.

Expanding Territory

In the last 40 years Islam has expanded its grip and moved to the West. Reza F. Safa in his book *Inside Islam* cites startling statistics. He writes, "In America, England, France, Holland and many other Western European countries the number of Muslims exceeds that of many religious minority groups. In some areas there are more Muslims than Christian denominational groups. George Otis, in his book *The Last Giants* points out the following information. In the United States, for instance, Muslims currently outnumber members of the Assemblies of God three to one. The United Kingdom now has more followers of Allah than Methodists and Baptists combined. In fact, Muslims are the nation's second-largest religious group, and have more adherents than all Protestant denominations put together."

Safa's alarming statistics continue: "In 1945, there was only one mosque in England. The number grew to 25 in 1950, to 80 by 1960, and to 200 mosques by 1976. By the year 1989, the number of mosques in England was more than 1,000. Three hundred of the buildings used for mosques were originally churches. Even the church that sent William Carey to India was converted to a mosque." And the numbers go on, including the rapid infiltration of Islam into the former Soviet Union, East and West Africa, and Kenya where their goal is to build one mosque for every 10 kilometers.

The most recent statistics provided by Jim Garlow, author of *A Christian's Response to Islam,* detail the continuing rise of Islam. One out of every four people in the world are Muslim. In America there are between 4 to 7 million devotees, which surpasses the second largest religious group, the Jews, at 6 million. According to projections released by the United Nations, 255 years into the millennium, 50 percent of all births will be to Muslim families.

> The question is not how to stop Islam from winning 50 million converts annually, but how to unmask the deception that has built its stronghold.

The world stands at the precipice of a social and cultural revolution. Samuel Huntington, former member of the National Security Council during the Carter Administration and author of *The Clash of Civilization,* projects an Islamic resurgence of staggering proportions. He believes the impact will be as great as that of the Protestant Reformation. Literally every aspect of culture will be changed.

Today, as in past years, youth is at the center of the revolution. Young adults between the ages of 18-24 are increasing by 20 percent. In Arab countries alone, there are 300 million below the age of 15. They make up 50 percent of the population and have become the agents of cultural change and social revolution.

The question is not how to stop Islam from winning 50 million converts annually, but how to unmask the deception that has built its stronghold and taken the ground of people's lives through deceit, division, inequality, immorality, violence, fear and, eventually...death. From these demonic roots the tree of Islam has grown and produced the fruit of destruction.

four

The Origins of Allah
The Meaning Behind the Name

The name Allah means submission and surrender. It implies total and complete devotion to a totalitarian god. It is the name of Islam—the religion of Mohammad.

What is behind the name of Allah? Is it just another name for God? Are Jehovah and Allah the same? Or does this god of Islam have different origins? Is he as C. Peter Wagner said in his *Global Prayer News,* "...No more God than is wormwood or Beelzebub or Appollyon or Shiva or Buddha or Baal or Lucifer. All of them are beings created by God, but who ended up agents of darkness, just as Satan did."

No God Except Allah

To Muslims, Allah is the name of the only god they serve. They exclaim, "La Elahe al Allah" and "Muhammad an Rasoul al Allah." Interpreted that means "There is no God except Allah" and "Muhammad is his prophet." Another translation reads, "There is no God who will be

31

worshiped except Allah" and "everyone must follow his prophet Muhammad."

Allah comes from the pre-Islamic name that combines the Arabic Al-ilah, meaning the god or deity, with the chief god of the more than 360 idols of Mecca. According to the *Arabic Lexiographical Miscellanies* by J. Blau in the Journal of Semitic Studies, Volume XVII, #2, "Al is the definite article 'the' and 'ilah' is an Arabic word for 'god.' It is not a foreign word. It is not even the Syriac word for God. It is pure Arabic."

Allat, the feminine form of the word, appears frequently among the "Theophorous names in inscriptions from North Africa," according to Dr. Arthur Jeffrey in his book *Islam: Muhammad, and His Religion*.

Even before the religion of Islam was born, Allah meant "the strength which characterized the desert warrior who, when faced with impossible odds, would fight to the death for his tribe."

Some historians have conjectured that Allah was derived from the mid-eastern word "el" which refers in the Ugaritic, Canaanite and Hebrew languages to either a true or false God. The Encyclopedia of Religion says Allah corresponds to one of the many "Babylonian gods."

The well-known Middle East scholar H.A.R. Gibb wrote in his book *Mohammedanism: An Historical Survey*, that Muhammad never had to explain who Allah was in the Quran because "...his listeners had already heard about Allah long before Muhammad was ever born." In fact, Arabs were pagans who recognized many different gods and goddesses. According to Middle East scholar E.M. Wherry, whose translation of the Quran is still used today, pre-Islamic Allah worship and the worship of Baal were both "astral religions and involved the worship of the sun, the moon and the stars."

Gods and Goddesses

Each tribe had their deity and nature gods. Archeologists have uncovered evidence of these tribal gods. Throughout the Middle East they have unearthed temples to the moon-god. From the mountains of

Turkey to the banks of the Nile the civilizations of the ancient world worshiped the moon-god.

The Sumarians worshiped a moon-god, symbolized by the crescent moon, whose names were Nanna, Suen and Asimbabbar. The Mesopotamians, Assyrians, Babylonians and the Akkadians all worshiped the moon-god. In ancient Syria and Canna, tribes followed the moon-god called Sin. The Sun goddess was the wife of Sin and the stars were their daughters.

From ancient texts to the Old Testament, the moon-god was mentioned. The Old Testament rebuked its worship in Deuteronomy 4:19, 17:3; 2 Kings 21:3-5, 23:5; Jeremiah 8:2, 19:13; and Zephaniah 1:5. From the excavation in Ur by Sir Leonard Woolley, to the 19th century finds by Amaud, Halevy and Glaser in Southern Arabia, the archeological evidence demonstrates the dominance of the cult of the moon-god.

> **The Sumarians worshiped a moon-god, symbolized by the crescent moon, whose names were Nanna, Suen and Asimbabbar.**

Allah was the god of the local Hasimite tribe—the tribe that Muhammad's father came from. Allah was known as the moon-god who had three daughters. And these daughters took on the role as intercessors between Allah and the people. Their names were Al-lat, Al-uzza, and Al-Manat.

Al-lat was the goddess of fate, a female counterpart to Allah. Al-uzza was the goddess of east Mecca. Human sacrifices were made to her. Islamic tradition tells the story of Muhammad's grandfather, Abdul Muttalib, who was the custodian of Ka'aba's 360 idols. He almost sacrificed his son, Abdullah, the servant of Allah and the father of Muhammad, to her. But a foreteller saved his life at the last moment. She then told Abdul to ransom his son for the price of 100 camels.

Pagan Roots

Even more evidence exists for the idolatrous and pagan roots of Allah.

His first two daughters had names which were the feminine equivalent of Hubal the chief god of the Ka'aba.

Ka'aba stood out from among the other 360 deities as a statue, a graven likeness of a man, made of red, precious stones and arms of gold. Literature and history both record the existence of Ka'aba and the Black Stone long before the emergence of Islam.

During pre-Islamic times it was called Beit-Allah or the House of Allah. When Mohammad drove the idols away he made one god to be the only god. He could have chosen the name of any of the other 359 dieties, but he choose Allah.

He kept the Ka'aba as a holy and sacred place and said that the Black Stone had the power to remove man's sins. He commanded every Muslim to make a pilgrimage to the stone at least once during his lifetime.

> **Mohammad took away all of the people's idols but one, Allah, and exalted that one as the "god" of Islam.**

Mohammad's attempt to create a monotheistic religion from a polytheistic one failed. He took away all of the people's idols but one, Allah, and exalted that one as the "god" of Islam. Those who had once prayed to Hubal in the Ka'aba, now prayed to Allah in the House of Allah.

Carlton S. Coon, who made many amazing archeological discoveries, was quoted as saying, "The god Il or Ilah was originally a phase of the moon-god." He went on to explain that "Similarly, under Muhammad's tutelage, the relatively anonymous Ilah became Al-Ilah, the God, or Allah, the Supreme Being."

In making this statement Coon underscored the fact that, to Mohammed, Allah was the "greatest" in the context of his polytheistic pagan beliefs. Muhammad was trying to side with the pagans and their belief in the moon-god Allah, and with the Jews and Christians in saying that, like Jehovah, Allah was the Supreme God. Muhammad's attempt at playing it both ways only fostered a falsehood that neither Jews or Christians accepted as the truth.

Dr. Newman who documented the early Christian-Muslim debates shared his findings stating, "Islam proved itself to be a separate and antagonistic religion which had sprung up from idolatry."

Mohammad transformed his one remaining idol into Allah and made him into a single being. Allah was stern, harsh and had compassion only on those who did what he said. His anger was released on those who could not or would not obey him.

Allah had no desire for love or fellowship. He had no interest in passing on his attributes and characteristics.

Unlike the God of the Old and New Testament, Allah had no need to reveal himself to man. It was impossible to know him in a personal way. None of his 99 names gave even a hint of a personal connotation. His entire relationship with man was through his will, the law and total obedience.

The God of Abraham?

Even though Muslims claim that Allah is the God of Abraham, Isaac and Jacob, and the same God that is recognized by both Jews and Christians, his name does not appear anywhere in the Torah—the first five books of the Old Testament. And, for that matter, it's not even mentioned anywhere else in the Bible.

Mecca, the city of Allah, and Medina are not among any of the cities in the Old Testament. If God's name was Allah, why didn't He give that name to Moses or any of His other prophets? Why didn't Jesus reveal that God had a different name?

In the words of Islamic scholar Caesar Farah, "There is no reason therefore to accept the idea that Allah passed to the Muslims from the Christians and Jews."

C. Peter Wagner amplifies this in his March 2002 *Global Prayer News:* "When Mohammed received a supernatural revelation that Allah was the one god who created the universe, you can be assured that such information did not come from the God of Abraham, Isaac and Jacob, who is also the Father of Jesus Christ."

Exchanging the Truth

What does God think of those who worship Allah? C. Peter Wagner, in his March 2002 edition of the *Global Prayer News,* said, "...It makes God mad! Romans 1:18-32 says the 'wrath of God is revealed' against those 'who exchanged the truth of God for a lie, and worshiped and served the creature rather than the Creator.' Make no mistake about it, Allah is not the Creator, he is a creature."

God is an eternal Being. His character and His name are without change. He told Moses "I AM that I AM" and identified Himself as eternal, unchangeable and without a beginning or an end. His definition of Himself left no room for another "god" or "idol."

When Jesus said He was the "I AM," He declared Himself to be the final, perfect and complete revelation of the One, true God. But Allah is not Jehovah, Yahweh or Elohim. Nor is he the great "I AM, that I AM." The god of Islam is not the God of the Bible. The God of Abraham, Isaac and Jacob is not the Allah that Muslims worship.

The Deception of Islam

Muslims are deceived by the lie that Allah is God. They believe that no other religion has a right to exist. There is no such thing as religious tolerance in Islam.

In countries around the world, Islam is not just a religion but a theocracy which rules society and allows for no separation between church and state. Opposition to Allah and Islam is not allowed. It is belief in Islam or death for those who refuse to believe or convert. Religious freedom does not exist.

When Islam moves into a country, a home or an individual's life it controls anything and everything. Allah demands submission and absolute obedience. There are no exceptions.

To Muslims, Islam involves all of their life. Safa puts it this way: "...Islam is a comprehensive, self-evolving system. It is the ultimate path of life, an ideology or system able to govern every political, economic, social and cultural aspect of their society, applicable to all times and places."

Few Muslims today know of the ancient and pagan origins of their religion. Even fewer Christians know about the idolatry behind the religion of the crescent moon. The Old Testament speaks often of the followers of Baal and their opposition and challenge to Jehovah and His people.

Baal, the male god of the Phoenicians and Canaanites, was the master, possessor and sun-god. His goddess, Ashtoreth, was his female counterpart.

Muslims are deceived by the lie that Allah is God. They believe that no other religion has a right to exist. There is no such thing as religious tolerance in Islam.

Members of the cult of Baal were promiscuous and lascivious. They participated in child sacrifice. They ate offerings left for the dead, and cut and mutilated themselves. Baal worshipers hated God and His elect.

Jezebel, the daughter of Ethbaal, was a devout worshiper and prophetess of Baal. She despised God's anointed prophets and opposed God with all that she had. She created an atmosphere of fear and torment throughout all of Israel.

The spirit that ushered in the worship of Baal in Phoenicia and Canaan, and later in Babylon, is the same spirit that raised Islam from the sands of Arabia. Hatred of God's elect and the spirits of immorality, fear, bloodshed, strife, division, and war are the attributes and characteristics of Islam and the worship of Allah.

How different they are from the character, nature and personality of the God they say they share with Jews and Christians. The One true God—Jehovah. The God of the Bible bares no resemblance to the character, nature and personality of the idol, Allah, that became the God of Islam.

five

The Doctrines of Islam
Etched in Stone

The Five Pillars of Islam read like a rulebook that leaves little room for deviation. Devoid of grace for its followers, it outlines the rituals, practices and affirmations that must be undertaken according to the exact letter of the law.

Touted by Muslims as the path to living a godly life, and the answer to the eternal questions of spirituality, the religious practices of Islam legislate a regimen of prayer, fasting, pilgrimage and charity. Their rituals are more about duty than devotion, law than love, and religion than relationship.

The Five Pillars

In attempting to keep the Five Pillars of Islam, Muslims are held to four degrees of performance that apply to everything they do from daily prayers to going to bed at night. These are: the Fard, which is required of all Muslims; the Wajib, which must be done every day by every

Muslim; the Sunnah, which is the example of the prophet Muhammad himself; and the Nafl, which refers to any actions that are extra or optional.

The definitions of the Five Pillars of Islam, or the Arkan al Islami, are:

Shahada—the declaration of allegiance to God
Salat—the ritual of daily prayers
Zakat—the ritual of annual charities
Saum—the ritual of month-long fasting
Hajj—the pilgrimage to Mecca

Keep in mind while we examine each of these pillars that Muslims believe that to neglect any of these is sin. Even though Islam does not believe in the doctrine of original sin of man, individuals can, through their negligence and disobedience to Allah, commit sin.

They believe individual sins and transgressions are recorded in a book of deeds by angels. And on the coming Day of Judgment, Muslims will give an answer for their lack of compliance and obedience to God's five-point program.

The Shahada—The Declaration of Faith

In Arabic the declaration is written, "Ashahadu an la ilaha ill Allah wa ashahadu anna Muhammadar Rasulullah." In English it is translated "I declare there is no god except God, and I declare that Muhammad is the Messenger of God." More than 1 billion Muslims say this Islamic Creed at least 17 times a day.

Believers in Islam recite this prayer to remind themselves that Allah is a reality in their lives. It is a way daily to answer the question in the Quran which asks, "Who will take a reminder?"

The Shahada or Declaration of Faith is that remembrance. The actual declaration underscores for the Muslim the belief that there should be no other god but Allah. Other gods can be anything that takes attention away from Allah.

Years ago the Taliban destroyed the ancient Buddha statues in the

Bamiyan Valley to eradicate graven images and false gods that were an affront to Allah. Their action was an example of the many lies and contradictions within Islam. Even though Islam decries idolatry in other religions, it refused to recognize the worship of false gods in its own.

> **Islam's declaration of worship of "one god alone" is a deception. Its claim of refusing to serve other gods is a glaring lie.**

Muhammad chose the idol Allah among 359 others to be the God of Islam. Yet he was not always consistent in his teaching or actions. He ordered the destruction of idols in Central and Southern Arabia, but allowed the statues of Jesus and the fire shrines of Zoroastrians to remain.

Islam's declaration of worship of "one god alone" is a deception. Its claim of refusing to serve other gods is a glaring lie.

The Salat—The Ritual of Daily Prayers

The second of the five pillars of Islam is regular, daily prayers or the salat.

To Muslims these prayers are considered more of a supplication than a simple prayer. They are rituals to show Allah that they are being obedient and attentive to his call.

The Quran encourages Muslims to pray and make supplication in Sura 47:19: "Therefore, you should know that there is no god but Allah; implore Him to forgive you your sins and to forgive the believing men and believing women; for Allah knows your activities and your resting places."

The Call to Prayer

Muslims cannot pray whenever they want to. Instead they are required to pray at five specific times throughout the day.

The first prayer begins at Fajr, or before sunrise. The next occurs at Zuhr, after the noon hour. At Asr, or in the late afternoon, they bow to pray again. Just after sunset, at Maghrib, they offer more supplications. And they end their day with their final prayers at Isha, or night.

During each of these prearranged times Muslims bow to Allah in prayer. They make supplications and say ready-made prayers or hadiths that help them ask Allah for everything from forgiveness to guidance, and success to healing from an illness.

But they cannot pray without first meeting seven preconditions. And these requirements must be met completely: They cannot pray to Allah at any time they want. They must give their supplication only during prayer time. Their hands, face and feet must be washed and ritually pure. They must be wearing clean clothes. They must pray in a clean place or in a mosque. No other place is acceptable. Men must be wearing pants and a shirt or a robe that covers their entire body. Women must also be fully clothed and wear a scarf or veil over their hair and face.

When they hear the call to prayer, they perform their prayers facing Mecca while bowing and prostrating themselves with their hands raised, palms up, in front of their body.

> **Muslims believe that if they are disobedient and fall behind in their prayers then all of their good deeds are ignored.**

The practice of sounding the call to prayer came after Muhammad considered many different ways to alert his people that it was time to gather. He thought about using bells, horns or drums, but a dream by one of his companions confirmed his choice.

The man had a dream and saw a man calling out phrases in a loud voice. He was declaring to people that it was time to come and pray. Muhammad saw the dream as a revelation and confirmation. The Muslim call to prayer, or azan, was born.

He ordered his companion to teach the words he had heard to a Muslim convert named Bilal. The African slave became the first muazzin, or person who calls the azan. He stood atop the wall of the mosque in Medina and cried out these words:

Allahu Akbar, Allahu Akbar.
Allahu Akbar, Allahu Akbar.

Ashahadu an la ilaha ill Allah.
Ashahadu an la ilaha ill Allah.
Ashahadu anna Muhammadar Rasulullah.
Ashahadu anna Muhammadar Rasulullah.
Haya alas Salah. Haya alas Salah.
Haya alal Falah. Haya alal Falah.
Allahu Akbar, Allahu Akbar.
La ilaha ill Allah.

The chant is translated from Arabic and means:

God is greater, God is greater.
God is greater, God is greater.
I declare there is no god but God.
I declare there is no god but God.
I declare Muhammad is the Messenger of God.
I declare Muhammad is the Messenger of God.
Rush to prayer. Rush to prayer.
Rush to success. Rush to success.
God is greater, God is greater.
There is no god, but God.

Muslims believe that their prayers at strategic times throughout the day keep them from breaking the laws of Allah. After all who wants to cheat on a business deal at 2 p.m., and ask Allah for a favor at 10 p.m.?

They also believe that Allah forgives their sins each time they pray. If they are negligent in their duty or pray irregularly they run the risk of being punished on the Day of Judgment. Before Allah weighs the good and the bad they have done, he first sees how often they have prayed. If they have been disobedient and have fallen behind in their prayers then all of their good deeds are ignored.

Prayer is not so much an act of devotion or dedication, but a way to escape the harsh judgment of Allah. It is a function of religion and not an expression of relationship.

The Zakat—The Ritual of Annual Charities

For many world religions, greed and gluttony top the list of the seven deadly sins. The love of money to the point of avarice or greed has often caused envy and hatred, and pitted the "haves" against the "have-nots."

Wars between the upper class and lower levels of society has produced many a revolution, created several ideologies and brought about all kinds of different social programs in hopes of curbing man's tendency to want to "keep up with the Jones" no matter what neighborhood they live in. Gluttony has also resulted in generations of people unable to control their urges to eat, engage in sex, and participate in drugs, alcohol and other vices. So Islam considers the two "g's" to be problems that must be addressed in the daily lives of Muslims.

Gift for the Poor

The Quran declares, "Allah has bought from the believers their lives and wealth and in exchange will give them Paradise." To comply with Allah's request, Islam combines a program of personal reform with physical action. Zakat, meaning poor-due or charity, is an annual ritual that helps Muslims to accumulate good deeds to ensure their entrance into Paradise.

Each year they set aside a portion of their wealth to be distributed to the poor. They engage in a month-long fast from their usual eating, drink and sexual activity. Zakat is the religious duty of everyone who meets certain requirements.

In order to participate, Muslims must have savings or assets to draw from that they can put aside for a year. Generally that is three ounces of gold or a business, car, animal, cash or even jewelry. Each man or woman must be past the age of puberty and free from insanity or other mental illness. In addition to the zakat, all other expenses and debts must be paid throughout the entire year.

If these conditions are met the zakat is 2.5 percent of a Muslim's average annual wealth. Payment can be arranged through a government agency, mosque or charitable organization.

The proceeds from zakat go to poor, needy and destitute Muslims. It can also be paid to those in debt, travelers in need of assistance, refugee foundations, widows or orphans.

In Islam, to refuse to pay zakat is to deny your brother. Not only is it a sin to do so, but one that comes with a stiff penalty. The Quran declares: "There are people who hide gold and silver to keep it and not to spend it in God's cause. Inform them of a painful punishment. On the day when the fire of Hell will be heated with the wealth they hid, they will be burned on their forehead with a branding iron and on their sides and back. They will be told, 'Here is the treasure that you hid for yourselves. Now taste the worth of what you hid'" (Sura 9:34-35). So according to Islam, there is no mercy for the sinner whose sin is refusal to pay zakat.

The Saum—The Ritual of Month-Long Fasting

Ramadan is a time of imposed fasting and also is the fourth pillar of Islam. This period of fasting comes in the ninth months of the Islamic lunar calendar and must be observed by all believers over the age of puberty. The chronically ill, elderly who are weak, and the mentally ill are exempt.

Muslims are required to abide by Ramadan's strict rules of fasting. For a period of 30 days they must observe the prescribed fast from dawn until dusk, eating only two meals—one before the sun rises and one just after sunset.

> In Islam, to refuse to pay zakat is only a sin, but one that comes with a stiff penalty.

To Muslims it is a time of struggle against their bodies and emotions. Their flesh must not win. They must not overeat or consume unhealthy foods. They are not allowed to take drugs, alcohol or smoke cigarettes. They also must not engage in sexual activity. They cannot use profanity, fight or lie from first light to sundown.

If they participate in any undesirable or forbidden behaviors, Allah will not recognize their fast. So severe is the punishment for disobedience that a Muslim who violates his or her fast may not go to Paradise. Once again, there is no grace for lawbreakers in Islam.

At the end of Ramadan there is a Festival of Fast Breaking or Eid ul Fitre. For the community and for Muslims it is a time for laughter and accomplishment for having made it through the 30 days of fasting.

It is customary for Muslims to give a small donation called a Sadaquat ul Fitr to their charity or Islamic center before the last day of Ramadan. While Muslims consider Ramadan to be a month of training, violations can make it a sentence of judgment and a ticket to Hell, not Paradise.

The Hajj—The Pilgrimage to Mecca

It is a religious gathering of massive magnitude. The Hajj, or the pilgrimage to Mecca, draws more than 2 million people to the desert city of Mecca where Muslims flock to the birthplace of Muhammad once each year.

Considered the journey of a lifetime, the ritual of Hajj has been undertaken by Muslims for over 14 centuries. They have come from nations all around the world and used various modes of transportation to reach the city and honor their prophet Muhammad.

The Hajj has three forms. I will not address each form separately, but merely mention the Tamattu, the Ifaad and the Uiran. The highest form of Hajj is considered the Tamattu. Only those truly devoted to Allah and who desire the Hereafter choose to participate in the Hajj. For a Muslim it is the highest form of worship.

Once pilgrims arrive for their 13-day pilgrimage, they head for the center of Mecca where the Ka'aba or Cube resides. It is a religious shrine made of bricks and covered with a heavy black cloth.

Muslims believe that Abraham brought Hagar, the handmaiden of Sarah, and their son, Ishmael, to this place. They believe that God instructed Abraham to leave Hagar and Ishmael in Arabia and return to Palestine.

Soon Hagar and her son ran out of food. They searched for something that would sustain them.

Praying for deliverance, Hagar collapsed in the center of the valley. Muslims believe that God answered her prayer and Ishmael struck his foot on the ground. When he did, water gushed forth. They would live and prosper.

When Abraham returned he would be required to sacrifice his son. Even though the biblical account states that God required Isaac as a sacrifice, Muslims believe that it was Ishmael whom God wanted placed on the altar. But instead of sacrificing his son, Abraham built a shrine in the Valley of Baca. The shrine became the city of Mecca.

Muhammad would be the prophet who, according to Muslims, cleaned up the city of its idolatry. Not so. Instead he chose one idol to be worshiped above the rest. He

> As captives to Islam, Muslims must "tow the line" imposed by the five pillars and doctrines or face the wrath of Allah. They must obey *all* or suffer eternal punishment.

called that one Allah after the deity of his tribe and he set the Black Stone of the Ka'aba as the place where he would be worshiped.

Legalistic Maneuvers

Just as with all the other pillars of Islam, participation in the Hajj has its set of stringent requirements. It is another legalistic maneuver of works motivated by the obsession to do anything and everything that will ensure entry into Paradise.

All along the way there are rules and regulations. There are timetables and restrictions that must be adhered to without deviation. It creates restrictions where Muslims do not know the meaning of freedom.

As captives to Islam, Muslims must "tow the line" imposed by the five pillars and doctrines or face the wrath of Allah. A slip here or a mistake there could send them to Hell. They must obey all or suffer eternal punishment.

The pilgrimage to Mecca must be done in the beginning of the Islamic month called Dhul Hjah. Muslims must be able to pay all of their debts and expenses for the journey. Those who are unable to afford the pilgrimage often decide to take a smaller journey called Umrah which can be done any time throughout the year. It doesn't count as pilgrimage to Mecca, but it can earn them extra merit with Allah.

Those who choose the main pilgrimage, or Hajj, must do all of the following: Men must wear two white garments know as Ihram. They are restricted clothes and stitching is not allowed in the cloth. It cannot have straps to join the two pieces of clothing together so it is worn like a toga. Women, however, have no clothing requirements and can wear whatever they like.

While observing Hajj, all pilgrims must observe the following: No sexual relations. No shaving or nail cutting. No wearing colognes, oils or scents of any kind. No killing of any living creatures or hunting of any kind. No fighting or arguing. No bathing or use of perfumed soaps.

When pilgrims arrive in Mecca they go to an entry station. It is the beginning of many steps in the ritual of Hajj that lasts several days.

Next the pilgrims bathe, change into their ritual clothing and a bus takes them from the station to the complex called Masjid al Haram—a huge building surrounding the holy place. In the center of the complex is the Ka'aba. It is covered with a black cloth called the Kiswah which is embroidered with verses from the Quran. Along the way, pilgrims chant a passage of scripture from the Quran that reminds them of why they are participating in the ritual of Hajj.

Once there, the pilgrims point to and kiss the Black Stone as an expression of their love for Abraham. They make seven trips around the fountain, or Well of Zam Zam, that saved Hagar and Ishmael. Then they move into a long chamber of two hills where they commemorate Hagar and her son's frantic search for food and water. They pray, study and reflect.

The next day the pilgrims travel to Mina where they give praise to Allah. They move on to the Plain of Arafah, a barren wasteland that represents the desolation of the Day of Judgment.

As night falls they travel to yet another place called Muzdalifah. There they gather together a number of small stones, just the right size for throwing. And the following day they travel back to Mina to a roofless enclosure.

Inside this enclosure are several tall stone pillars. The pilgrims gather together, take the stones they collected the night before and throw them at the pillars. This represents the stoning of the devil, Shaytan, who convinced Abraham not to sacrifice his son.

Then a group of pilgrims, maybe five to 10, offer the sacrifice of an animal. And they slaughter the animal according to the Islamic tradition.

Their knife must be sharp so that they can cut the animal's jugular vein swiftly. They must make sure that no other animals are near when the sacrifice is taking place, and the animal being sacrificed must feel no pain or sense any fear.

The pilgrims then eat the flesh of the animals they have sacrificed. Any meat that is leftover is taken to local meat processing plants where it is canned and given to the poor to eat.

But the pilgrimage is still not over.

For the men, the next step is to shave their head. By doing so they signify their rebirth into the "true" faith of Islam. Women are not required to shave their heads, but instead to cut off a lock of hair.

After the ritual of shaving, the pilgrims are released from the restrictions of the Hajj. So they return to Mecca and spend the next few days around the Ka'aba, stoning the Shaytan, or praying and studying.

On the last day of the Hajj they make one more set of passes around the Ka'aba. They ask Allah for forgiveness and their Hajj is complete. The next day they will celebrate the Eid ul Adha, or the Festival of the Sacrifice.

Ticket to Paradise

The Five Pillars of Islam are a reflection of man's attempt to earn his way to Paradise. But nowhere in Islam is there a place for grace. Man is doomed to keep the law perfectly or perish trying to cross every "t" and dot every "i."

Like the Pharisees of Jesus' day, Muslims are blinded by the bondage of the law. The religious spirits that are so critically a part of

Islam keep their followers in chains and unable to break free to experience the freedom that salvation, deliverance and healing brings.

It is the futility of Muslim laws, rituals and regulations that causes young men to give their lives as suicide bombers. They believe the means justify the ends as they ensure a quick ticket to paradise and its fleshly excesses.

So great is the deception that now many young women who think they have no hope of paradise, are doing the same. As Paul says in 2 Corinthians 4:3-4, "But even if our gospel is veiled, it is veiled to those who are perishing, whose minds the god of this age has blinded, who do not believe, lest the light of the gospel of the glory of Christ, who is the image of God, should shine on them." And in verse 6 he writes, "For it is the God who commanded light to shine out of darkness, who has shone in our hearts to give the light of the knowledge of the glory of God in the face of Jesus Christ."

When the deception of the doctrine of false and errant teaching is exposed in Islam, Muslims will finally be able to experience what many of us have already encountered. We have come to know the One true God and His Son Jesus. For "He has delivered us from the power of darkness and conveyed us into the kingdom of the Son of His love, in whom we have redemption through His blood, the forgiveness of sins" (Colossians 1:13-14).

When that day comes they will know the freedom from the bondage of centuries past. They will experience the joy that comes with the love, grace and acceptance from the heart of God Himself.

six

The Quran

Scribes Aside

Islam is a complex and confusing religion, only complicated more by the contradictions of the Quran and the teachings of Muhammad. Not only do the holy scriptures of Muslims contain many errors concerning the people, places, historical and chronological events in the Old and New Testaments, but its 114 Suras, or chapters, weren't written down by Muhammad at all.

Because of Muhammad's illiteracy, his followers wrote down his revelations as they heard him recite the verses. Then after Muhammad's death, his scribes translated his teachings into Arabic and put them in what is known today as the Quran.

Coincidentally, 60 to 70 percent of Muslims who are not Arabs cannot read the Quran, even today. Only a handful of Muhammad's followers have actually read and understand his teachings.

The Word of Allah

Despite this fact, the Quran is considered by all Muslims to be Allah's word. It is considered a holy book that is respected and revered by every follower. It doesn't seem to matter to Muslims that the Islamic scripture is confusing, repetitive and contains many contradictions that are hard to explain.

Far from inspired, the Quran was revised frequently by Muhammad's scribes to justify his behavior and questionable acts. Muhammad often used his so-called prophetic revelations to give acceptability to his sexually immoral acts. He covered his sin, created deception and fostered a doctrine of the demonic in the name of holy writ.

Even though Muslim scholars claim that the god of the Quran is the God of the Bible, the two scriptures bear no resemblance to each other.

Safa, the author of *Inside Islam,* cites the opinion of the Muslim scholar Ib-Ishaq. He details the chronological order of the Quran in this way: "Creation; Adam and Eve; Noah and his issue; Hud; Salih; Abraham; Lot; Job; Shuayb; Joseph; Moses; Ezekiel; Elijah; Elisha; Samuel; David; Solomon; Sheba; Isaiah; al-Khidr; Daniel; Hananiah; Azariah; Mishael and Ezra; Alexander; Zecharia and John; the family of Imran and Jesus, son of Mary; the Companion of the Cave; Jonah; the Three Messengers; Samson; George."

You might be wondering, like I did, who Hud is. How about Alexander? And Salih, Sheba, Shuayb and al-Khidr don't look familiar.

What about the Companion of the Cave? Who's that? The Three Messengers? And who is George? The Quran is hardly a mirror image of the Holy Bible, the Word of God.

No Salvation

Let's look for a minute at some other glaring problems with the teachings of Muhammad which are recorded in the Quran. If you ask most Christians about sin, they will tell you that God has forgiven them and put their sin as far as the east is from the west. But if you ask a Muslim the same question, you're likely to get a shoulder shrug and a quick response of "Who knows?"

There is in fact no promise of salvation for the Muslim. There isn't even the word salvation in the Quran.

Sura 13:22-23 says, "Those who avert evil with good theirs shall be the ultimate abode, Gardens of Eden which they shall enter; and those who were good to their parents and wives and their seed." It's all about good works for the Muslim. There is no concept of grace.

Far from inspired, the Quran was revised frequently by Muhammad's scribes to justify his behavior and questionable acts.

If a Muslim's good deeds are more than his bad deeds, he might get to Heaven. But even that is questionable to a Muslim. There is no loving God offering the gift of salvation in Islam. Everything is subject to the whim of an angry and harsh deity—Allah.

Muslims know nothing of a loving God. The Quran mentions 24 times that Allah has no love for the sinner, only love for those that fear him. Faith in Allah brings no assurance of forgiveness of sin, salvation or eternal life.

In Islam sin exists, but cannot be forgiven. Therefore Muslims must find a way to justify their sin. Muhammad frequently did this himself, then he changed the Quran, after the fact, to cover his own sin of taking his adopted son's wife.

Unlike in Christianity, Islam views adultery and fornication as merely temporary marriages subject to the sexual desires of the man. A man can take any woman as his wife at any given time and for any length of time.

As a matter of fact it is a common practice for a married Muslim man to take another woman as his temporary wife while traveling away from home. Muhammad had 14 wives and two mistresses.

The Real Truth

The average Muslim doesn't really know about the teachings of Muhammad or the verses of the Quran. Because of their high rates of illiteracy, they cannot read or write for themselves. So they often depend on others to interpret scripture for them, and they also lean heavily on stories, myths and legends about Muhammad and his life.

As I mentioned earlier, many Muslims cannot read the Arabic language. For most, Arabic is a foreign language. There are 22 Arab nations around the world and nearly 1.4 billion Muslims. Of that number, only 20 percent are Arabic. That means most or possibly all of the other 80 percent cannot read, write or speak Arabic.

Imagine if most of the Christians in the world couldn't read their Bibles. We would be as deceived as those who

Is it any wonder then that Muslims are so deceived? They are unable to discern light for themselves.

practice Islam. We would have to depend on others—theologians, preachers, ministers—to do our reading and interpreting for us. We would have to trust them to tell us the truth. And we would have little chance to know the real truth about God.

Is it any wonder then that Muslims are so deceived? They have to depend on their clerics and the caliphates of Muhammad for the interpretation of Islam's religious and moral principles. They are unable to discern light for themselves.

Without light, they walk in darkness. And how great is that darkness.

seven

The Caliphs
Guardians at the Gate

I slam, which started out as a small sect, had grown into a major Arab power. Within a generation it was transformed into an empire. By two or three generations it expanded its influence to include three continents and many different cultures.

But the death of Muhammad in 632 threatened Islam's continued existence. After his death, Muslims had a few decisions to make.

For nearly 23 years Muhammad had guided them. His followers thought they had found the answer they were looking for. He had been the one they looked to for their spiritual, legal and moral direction. Now he was gone.

Who would take his place? Would Islam fall apart? How would it survive?

"Muhammad is no more than a Messenger. Many were the Messengers who passed away before him. If he dies or is killed, will you turn and run?" (Quran 3:144). So they elected a new leader as

Muhammad's successor. But the manner in which that successor was chosen is still a source of debate between today's Shiites and Sunnis.

The Shiites believed the successor should have been Muhammad's blood relative. Sunnis held that the supreme leader of Islam should be elected by consensus.

The Successors

One matter was without debate: Islam required a successor to survive. So they put in place a caliphate, supreme leader and successor to the prophet Muhammad.

Under Muhammad, the Muslim State was a theocracy. He was the sole authority and the Sharia, the religious and moral principles of Islam, were the law of the land. So caliphates were not just religious leaders, but secular rulers as well.

Four caliphs ruled during the next 30 years. They called the time frame Khulafa or Rashidah and the Period of the Rightly Guided Caliphs because these first rulers stuck closely to the teachings of the Quran and to Muhammad's teaching.

The first caliphate was Abu Bakr As-Sadeeq. He was not, however, the first choice of many.

Medina converts suggested one from their own camp for election. A heated debate ensued as to the most qualified.

Finally, Abu Bakr As-Sadeeq from Mecca was chosen. He was one of Muhammad's closest friends and led prayers at the main mosque when the prophet was ill. He would be responsible for uniting all of the tribes under Islam's rule. But his reign would be short—just two years and three months. Marked by rebellion and conflict, it ended with his death.

Shortly before he died, he called a council of the remaining companions of the prophet and discussed who should rule after him. He suggested Umar ibn al Khattab. They agreed. Umar was elected as the new caliph in a public vote.

As the second caliph, Umar spearheaded the expansion of Islam. His 10-year term brought growth that continued for a hundred years.

His armies defeated the Persians and Byzantine empires. They occupied what today is Iraq and Iran, and moved into Central Asia and the Punjab. His troops conquered all the Asiatic territories with the exception of what is modern Turkey. They also moved northward and took possession of Syria and Damascus. They extended their control into North Africa, Europe and most of Spain.

Reza Safa sums it up this way: "Within a hundred years after Muhammad's death, Islam became an empire in which Allah and the laws of Islam ruled from the Punjab to the Pyrenees, and from Samakand to the Sahara."

> **Problems began to arise. Corruption crept into Uthman's administration. Opposition began to spread. His governors became rebellious.**

Umar helped to bring greater organization to the Muslim government by dividing it into eight provinces. Each was ruled by governors that were appointed by the caliph. He also reformed the tax system and the treasury. But all of his successes could not stave off a Persian assassin who ended his life.

As he lay dying he appointed a committee to choose his successor. Together they chose Uthman ibn Affan, another trusted companion of the prophet.

Under Uthman's administration, Islam progressed rapidly. He ordered the building of the Muslim navy. And under his direction an official copy of the Quran was made available in every Muslim city.

Problems, however, began to arise. Corruption crept into his administration. Opposition began to spread. His governors became rebellious.

As upheaval continued, a group of dissidents came to talk to Uthman regarding their displeasure with the governors' rule. He heard their concerns and promised action.

On the way back to their province, a saboteur placed a letter among their belongings. The letter threatened the murder of the governors.

The signature was assumed to be Uthman's. Instead, it was a forgery.

Angry, the caravan returned to Medina and confronted Uthman. Refusing to believe that he had not written the letter, the angry mob surrounded him and put him to death.

The fourth caliph was Ali ibn Abi Talib. Selected by a vote of the people, after Uthman's death, he faced the same problems as his predecessor.

What was he to do about the rebellious governors in Iraq, Egypt and Syria? On top of that problem, pressure was mounting for him to investigate Uthman's murder. He refused to bring the murderers to justice.

> The struggle for power grew more intense and finally resulted in civil war. That war continues today throughout the Muslim world.

Angered by his decision, dissidents tried to force his hand. They wanted the killers punished.

Escalating Tensions

Tensions continued to escalate within the Muslim community. Resistance to Ali was mounting. The struggle for power grew more intense and finally resulted in civil war. That war continues today throughout the Muslim world.

In the midst of all the turmoil and after many battles, Ali was assassinated. In the year 661, a Kharanjite stabbed him to death after his morning prayers.

Ali was the last of the true caliphs who lived by Muhammad's precepts. After his death, the caliphate system was never the same again.

Following a string of three political assassinations, the people no longer had a voice in the leadership of Islam. The balance of power had shifted. The political structure of Islam would never again be the way it had been in Medina.

eight

By Blood and the Sword

Beyond the Facade

t's a disturbing picture that we have seen a lot since September 11, 2001. There he is. Osama bin Laden with an AK-47 by his side, appearing quite peaceful as a holy man sitting in front of a wall of books. Is he a holy man? Is he a scholar?

The distorted picture he presents might get clearer if we pull off the mask and reveal the true face of Islam. Behind Bin Laden and the tenets of Islam is a terrorist agenda. Like others who practice Jihad, he is dedicated not to a peaceful religion, but to one that has a history of blood and the sword.

Worldwide Terrorism

We've seen the pictures before. But the rap sheet for worldwide terrorism didn't begin on September 11 with the planes that destroyed the Twin Towers in New York City, and crashed into the Pentagon and a Pennsylvania field. In 1979, unprecedented violence spread across North Africa and the Middle East perpetrated by Muslim fundamentalists.

Then later in 1979, a group of Muslim students seized the U.S. embassy in Iran. They held 52 Americans hostage for 444 days. That same year in Pakistan, a group of Muslim fundamentalists torched the U.S. Embassy. And in 1982, it happened again.

In Lebanon, 37 Americans and Westerners were taken hostage by Hezbollah. Nine years later the last American was finally freed.

In 1983, three suicide bombs hit Beirut leaving the American Embassy and the U.S. and French barracks in rubble. Three-hundred and fifty people were killed including 241 U.S. Marines. Hezbollah claimed responsibility.

In 1985, they struck again when they highjacked a TWA jetliner to Beirut.

In 1988, a different Islamic group claimed responsibility for the downing of a Pan Am jet over Scotland. All 259 passengers were killed.

During the 1980s alone nearly 100 foreigners were kidnapped in Lebanon by Hezbollah. At least eight

> **Even as the death toll began to rise from terrorist acts, some still believed that Islam was a bloodless and peaceful religion.**

of those were later killed, including three Americans. But the reign of terror and the shedding of innocent blood wasn't over.

In February 1993, a bomb rocked the Twin Towers of the World Trade Center killing six people and injuring more than 1,000. Abdel Rahman and 14 of his followers were arrested, charged and given life in prison for their part in the bombing. The indictment against them read, "They unlawfully, willfully and knowingly combined, conspired, confederated and agreed together and with each other to levy a war of urban terrorism against the United States."

Even as the death toll began to rise from terrorist acts, some still believed that Islam was a bloodless and peaceful religion. They would find out once again that Jihad wasn't just a struggle against the lusts of the flesh, but an all-out war against all the "infidels" around the world.

Jihad—War to the Infidels

If you consult the Internet or some textbooks you'll discover a watered-down version of the word "Jihad." Pro-Islamic writers will tell you it means "a struggle or striving to work toward something with complete determination." They concede that it is a "war" of sorts against evil and wrongdoing. It is an act of fighting or any act that promotes the cause of Allah and creates justice on the earth.

They might even mention that Jihad continues until all the evil is removed or the other side cries "uncle." The Quran puts it this way: "Let those fight in the Cause of God who sell the life of this world for the next life. To the one who fights in the Cause of God, whether he is killed or achieves victory, We shall soon give him a great reward. And why shouldn't you fight in the Cause of God and of those who, being weak, are mistreated; the men, women and children whose only cry is, 'Our Lord! Save us from this land whose people are oppressors and bring to us from You someone who will protect us and bring to us from You someone who will help.' Those who believe fight in the Cause of God, and those who reject faith fight in the cause of evil. So fight against the friends of Shaytan" (Sura 4:74-76).

What they don't tell you is that they believe the "evil" or "infidels" are all who do not serve and worship Allah. And that death awaits those who refuse to convert.

Fear is their strongest tactic to win and keep converts. "When the sacred months are past, kill those who join other gods wherever you find them, and seize them, beleaguer them, and lie in wait for them with every kind of ambush; but if they convert and observe prayer and pay the obligatory alms, let them go their way" (Quran 9:5).

The Cry for Bloodshed

The friends of Shaytan are anyone who does not believe in Allah. So a

Jihad isn't a struggle to overcome the evil desires of the flesh for sex, drugs and a favorite food. Make no mistake about it, Jihad is a call to bloodshed and murder.

Maybe this statement by Sheikh Mohammed Yazbeck during a rally in Baalbeck a week after the bombing of a U.S. Marines headquarters in Lebanon will clarify this point. He threatened, "Let America, Israel and the world know that we have a lust for martyrdom and our motto is being translated into reality."

New York City, Washington, D.C., Pennsylvania and the rest of the United States of America know all too well what he means. The article "Horror & Heroes: What Really Happened on Flight 93" in the *Newsweek* December 3, 2001, edition recounts the story of the lead terrorist on the fated airliner.

Ziad Samir Jarrah sat in seat 1B. He had received his final instructions the night before from the ringleader, Mohamed Atta. He bathed carefully and shaved all of his excess body hair. While he sat waiting to

> War, division, revenge and retaliation follow Islam everywhere it spreads. It creates hatred, brings sorrow and leaves behind mourning and confusion.

carry out his part of this evil mission he probably prayed, "There is no God but God." He was heading for Paradise, the reward for the deed he was about to commit.

Days before, he wrote his girlfriend in Germany. He told her he wouldn't be back, but wrote, "You should be proud because it is an honor and in the end you will see that everyone will be happy."

At that moment his thoughts were of the martyr's reward that Atta had promised. Atta wrote: "This is the day, God willing, you spend with the women of Paradise."

According to the Quran, Ziad would receive all he could eat and drink in a bedroom set aside for him and him alone. At his bed would be four, perpetual virgins waiting to fulfill his every desire. Because of his act of Jihad, he would receive 70 more virgins. Such was the reward of the martyr. For the religion of "peace," it was payment in full for unspeakable violence in the name of Allah.

Blood trails throughout the entire history of Islam. War, division, revenge and retaliation follow it everywhere it spreads. It creates hatred, brings sorrow and leaves behind mourning and confusion. The bloodthirsty spirit of Islam is clearly exposed in this statement by Hussein Musawi, the leader of the Islamic Amal movement. It is printed in the book *Inside Islam* by Reza F. Safa: "This path is the path of blood, the path of martyrdom. For us death is easier than smoking a cigarette if it comes while fighting for the cause of God and while defending the oppressed."

Even in the Muslim stronghold of Iran, blood flowed in the streets. The Ayatollah began cracking down on the fundamentalist group the Mojahedin in 1981. His military and revolutionary police started their executions in June. By December they had murdered 2500 Mojahedin followers, some by hanging and others killed at the hands of firing squads. They were merely fulfilling the mandate to wash blood with blood.

The Mojahedin launched their own assault, assassinating high-ranking government officials daily. They killed hundreds, blowing them to pieces using suicide bombers. The assassins were young men, age 15 to 25.

The bloodshed continued for four solid years and took the lives of more than 12,000 dissidents, the majority of whom were Mojahedin. Every assassination, killing, murder and suicide was a show of devotion to their heroes—Muhammad and Hussein, his grandson the Sayyad al-Shudada, lord of the martyrs.

To the Shiite there is no way for justice to be done except through the shedding of blood.

The Highest Honor

To Muslims dying and killing in the name of Allah is a supreme honor. It is the highest way to please Allah. It is the only real way of receiving eternal life.

That's why so many young men volunteer to be basiji or the mobilized. They are willing to throw their bodies on landmines, run into high voltage border fences and take on any suicide mission. When some sign up they are only 12 or 13. Lured by the promise of behesht or Paradise they are willing to do anything for the key that unlocks the gate to Heaven.

But look beyond the facade and see the real image of Islam. It is not restricted to the Shiite faction alone or to what many call the "fanatic fringe." The face of violence, militancy and bloodshed covers all of Islam. It goes deep into its roots. "O Prophet, strive hard against the unbelievers and the hypocrities, and be fire against them. Their abode is Hell, an evil refuge indeed" (Quran 9:73).

Terror, fear and death are the modus operandi of Islam. Their centuries old vengeance against the injustice of the Crusades, and their hatred against the United States for its stand with Israel, fuels the fires of bloodshed. Only the blood of Jesus offers Muslims the hope they are looking for.

> Islam holds its followers in bondage. They are caged by a deception that can only lead them to death and the wrath of Allah.

Paul wrote to the Hebrew Church, "Inasmuch then as the children have partaken of flesh and blood, He Himself likewise shared in the same, that through death He might destroy him who had the power of death, that is, the devil, and release those who through fear of death were all their lifetime subject to bondage" (Hebrews 2:14-15).

Islam holds its followers in bondage. They are captives to the twisted thinking of the tenets of their religion. They fear not only Allah and his wrath, but also the devil and his demons. They are caged by a deception that can only lead them to death and the wrath of Allah.

nine

Paradise

Lost or Found

Nearly every society and culture has some concept of the afterlife. Whether it's Heaven, Valhalla, Nirvana or Paradise, it's a place where followers reap their eternal rewards.

That's where the comparison ends. Heaven, Islam style, doesn't even come close to the biblical view of God's third Heaven habitation where believers worship God in holiness, love and joy.

For Muslims, entry into Paradise isn't the result of salvation or a personal relationship with God and His Son. You can't get through the gates of Heaven if you are just anyone—especially if you're a woman. Paradise is an Islamic men's club. No women are allowed, that is, except for the virgins that spend all of eternity satisfying the lustful and insatiable desires of their male masters.

Sex and Paradise

The Voice of the Martyrs magazine quotes the opinion of Sheikh Sha'rawi, the most renowned Sheikh in the Arab and Islamic countries, on Muhammad's view of Paradise. He said, "The apostle of God was asked, 'Will we have sexual intercourse in Paradise?' He said, 'Yes, I swear by the One who holds my soul in His hand that it will be a vigorous intercourse, and as soon as the man departs from her (the houri) she will again become immaculate and virgin.'"

Sha'rawi added, "The apostle of God, Muhammad, said, 'Every morning one hundred virgins will be (the portion) of each man.'"

> No one gets to Paradise as soon as they die. They have to go through the Last Day, then the judgment, a long, drawn-out process.

Muhammad leaves no question unanswered about the sexual privileges of men in Heaven. They will choose as many women as they desire. Women, however, if they make it to Paradise at all, are forced to choose between the husband they had on earth when they died or, if they were divorced, the husband of their choice. But no one gets to Paradise as soon as they die.

Judgment Day

Before any Muslim can get to Paradise, they have to go through the Last Day. On that particular day all living beings die including the angels. After that comes the judgment which is a long, drawn-out process.

First each person stands in line and waits their turn. There is no eating, drinking or sleeping—just waiting.

When it's your turn to step forward and be judged, two angels escort you before Allah. He decides if you have been good or not. If you get the record of your deeds in your right hand then you have done well. If your record is put in your left hand you're in trouble.

Every Muslim's faith is thoroughly examined. Witnesses are called to give an account. Lying is not tolerated. Even calling out to idols for help is pointless.

As you continue to stand before Allah at the judgment, your prayer life is examined for negligence and disobedience. Then all of your good and bad deeds are weighed. Allah explains everything to you about how he has seen your life. Then he delivers your verdict.

Rather than being the end of the process, the verdict only moves you to the next stage—the Plain of Judgment. There you overlook the pit of Hell. You can see the deep hole, watch the flames rising and feel the intense heat.

If you've been a terrible sinner, angels immediately throw you in the pit for a period of torment. All that remains are the guilty or innocent who now must go over the bridge called the Sirat that stretches across the chasm of Hell and leads to Paradise.

The Sirat is as thin as a razor and has jagged edges and spikes. If you were a righteous person or prophet you will quickly make it across the bridge and into Paradise. If you were a good person you'll get to the other side, but you'll suffer some cuts and bruises. If your good and bad deeds were about equal, you could end up in a spot between Heaven and Hell called the Heights.

The rest of the sinners along the bridge will only make it half way across and then fall perilously into the pit of Hell. There they will be tormented by jinni, or evil spirits, and will have no way of escape. Allah created Hell for both the righteous and the unrighteous. In the Quran, Sura 15:43-44, it is described this way: "Gehanna (hell) shall be their promised land all together. Seven gates it has, and unto each gate a set portion." *The Voice of the Martyrs* magazine quotes Al Baidawik, a commentator on the levels of Hell: "It has seven gates through which they will be admitted for their great number. The layers they will descend according to their rank are, respectively: Gehanna, the highest is for the rebellious monotheists; the second, Al Laza (furnace) is for the Jews; the third is Al Hutama (the crushed) which is for the Christians; the fourth is Al-Sa'ir (the blaze) for the Sabaeans; the fifth, Saqar (scorching heat) is for the fire worshipers; the sixth is hell which is for the unbelievers; and the seventh is the Pit for the deceivers."

For those residing in the levels of Hell, the greatest torment is not knowing whether or not you will be allowed to someday go to Heaven. For Muslims, not everyone will spend all of eternity in Hell, some will complete their time of punishment and be sent to Heaven.

Reward of the Faithful

What is the Islamic view of Heaven? It is called Paradise or Jumnah, and is created for those who have listened to their fitrah or inner nature, and lived a life of faith and good deeds. At the entrance to Heaven is a wall with eight gates. Each of the gates is named after a religious ritual established on the earth. Some get to choose the gate they want to walk through, but most do not.

Heaven consists of seven layers and contains homes. Each person is assigned a level that depends on the good deeds they have performed. You can visit friends and family on different levels even though you can't live with them.

Once in your home, special servants and pleasure mates called houris provide endless, guiltless sex—a benefit of the Islamic Heaven, if you are a man. If you're a woman, you are the servant. Wine and the best foods are in unlimited supply. The vices you could not partake of on earth are now yours to enjoy for all eternity.

No Equality

For the Muslim man Paradise is found. For the woman it is lost. Muhammad said, "I was shown the Hell-fire and that the majority of its dwellers are women."

By their prophet's own admission, Islamic women will never share in Heaven's questionable rewards. Instead women are the perpetual virgins, the goddesses of an idolatrous religion who offer sexual favors on the altar of abomination for all eternity.

It's difficult to believe that any religion, especially one claiming to share its God with Judaism and Christianity, could be so brazen to refuse a whole segment of society the rewards of their deity's presence. The God of the Bible, Who is both male and female, created a universe where the man and woman are equals, co-rulers. He placed both of them in authority and gave them dominion in the earth. The only difference in His man was this: one had a womb and the other didn't.

Allah sees no such equality. His concept of Heaven is more a view of Hell than a vision of Paradise.

No Heaven

Those who practice Islam have no concept of the Heaven that Jesus taught. He spoke of the habitation of God where there is no marriage, death, sorrow, pain, curse, night or wickedness. There, throughout all of eternity, will be joy, rest, peace, righteousness and the unmatched glory of God. And in the presence of God, those who have been forever changed by His Spirit and power will receive the fullness of their inheritance and the rewards for their service.

Muhammad said, "I was shown the Hell-fire and that the majority of its dwellers are women."

Jesus said in John 14:1-3, "Let not your heart be troubled; you believe in God, believe also in Me. In My Father's house are many mansions; if it were not so, I would have told you. I go to prepare a place for you. And if I go and prepare a place for you, I will come again and receive you to Myself; that where I am, there you may be also." This is the promise for all those who believe.

Heaven has no gender restrictions. Men and women are both welcome. There is no age requirement and no racial discrimination. All people of every race and country are welcome. The only entry requirement is a personal, life-changing, transformational relationship with Jesus, the Only Son of God. He is "the way, the truth, and the life" (John 14:6) and the only key that unlocks the door to the gate of Heaven.

ten

The Gender War

A Question of Value

They are victims of rape, sexual assault and domestic violence. They have been murdered, burned, disfigured, beaten, tortured and sexually mutilated. They have been killed in the name of honor, and no one has stopped the men who have murdered them.

They are the wives of Islamic men. They are the causalities of a gender war. They are the women of Islam.

In an urgent petition to the United Nations, signers called for immediate action against Madhu, the government of Afghanistan. They cited consistent rights violations including: "Stoning women in public for not wearing their burqua, or the proper attire, including simply not having the mesh covering in front of their eyes."

For their infraction, one woman was beaten to death by an angry mob. She had accidentally exposed her arm while driving a car. Another woman was stoned to death for trying to leave the country with a man who was not a relative.

Rights Violation

The Idiot's Guide to Understanding Islam presents quite a different view. Presently a biased representation of Muslim life, they paint a civilized picture of equality for women. They list these protected rights of women: "A man's property cannot be seized by her husband. Women cannot be denied the right to an education. Ruining a woman's reputation is a criminal act. Forced marriage is prohibited. Women can file legal suits in court and provide sole testimony. Women can initiate divorce. Women get automatic custody of young children after divorce. Alimony and palimony are mandatory. Women can enter into contracts without interference. Spousal abuse is a punishable offense. Women receive equal pay for equal work. Women can vote and stand for office."

What an insult to Islamic women around the world. They have no property of their own. They can pursue an education, but are never allowed to use it. They are beaten for misbehavior, but never live to fight for their reputation. They are married and divorced at the whim of the men around them. They are paid alimony and palimony to pave the way for the next wife. They are subjected to marriages they never asked for. They are beaten and killed by husbands who get away with it in the name of "honor." They can never receive equal pay because they are not allowed to work. And they can vote, but face sure opposition if they pursue their rights.

You judge for yourself whether women are treated fairly.

Discrimination Begins Early

The discrimination begins at an early age. In many Islamic countries, the government provides free transportation. Each day children wait for the buses to take them to school.

I have watched as children stood by the road waiting for the bus to arrive. The bus stops and the doors open. The young girls stand back and allow the boys to get on the bus first. Once the boys are inside, the bus driver closes the doors and drives off, leaving the girls by the roadside.

This is only the tip of the iceberg of inequality and prejudice uniformly practiced by Islam. So severe is the treatment of women due to the tenets of the religion that they are not allowed to work or go out in public without a male relative.

Professional women such as professors, translators, doctors, lawyers, artists and writers have been forced from their jobs and restricted to their homes. Because they cannot work, women often starve to death or have to beg in the streets, even if they are highly educated professionals.

Residences where a woman is present must have painted windows so that the women inside cannot be seen. Women must wear shoes that are considered silent so that they are never heard. And they live in constant fear for their lives for committing the slightest misbehavior.

Women as Playthings

The rights of women are violated daily in the name of Islam. Husbands have the power of life and death over their women relatives, especially their wives. All men have the right to stone or beat a woman to death for exposing even an inch of her flesh or for offending them in any way.

To Islamic men, women are subhuman and are no more than property to be taken and discarded at will. Even the prophet Muhammad said, "Wives are playthings, so take your pick."

> **The rights of women are violated daily in the name of Islam. Husbands have the power of life and death over their women relatives, especially their wives.**

To Muslim men, women are "toys." Muhammad fostered this view that has been perpetuated by caliph after caliph. In his book *Al-Musanaf* quoted in *The Voice of the Martyrs* magazine, Abu Bakr Ahmed Ibn Abd Allah, one of the many Muslim scholars, was quoted as saying about a conversation between Umar the Just Caliphate and one of his wives: "You are a toy, if you are needed we will call you." Amru bin Al added his own comment: "Women are toys, so choose."

The woman's position in Islamic society is subject to her husband

and the other men in the culture. She is not an equal with rights, but is considered inferior. The man has authority and superiority over the woman. The Quran in Sura 4:34 states, "Men have authority over women because Allah has made the one superior to the other."

Ahmed Zaki Tuffaha in his book *The Woman and Islam* is quoted in *The Voice of the Martyrs* as saying, "God established the superiority of men over women by the verse Sura 4:34 which prevents the equating of men and women. For here man is

Muslims marry women, make temporary contracts and divorce them at will. Women have no voice, no will and no rights even to their own bodies.

above the woman due to his intellectual superiority."

This is a far cry from the biblical view of women. The Apostle Paul wrote in Galatians 3:28, "There is neither Jew nor Greek, there is neither slave nor free, there is neither male nor female; for you are all one in Christ Jesus."

For Muslim women such equality is an impossibility. Not only are women considered to be inferior and valued only for their sexual abilities, but also various clerics and scholars represent them as deficient in intelligence, religion and gratitude.

The Deficiencies of Women

The magazine *The Voice of the Martyrs* cites Sahih Al Bukhari and his scholarly works. Other than the Quran, Bukhari's opinion is considered, even by other Muslims, to be the most authentic representation of their beliefs other than that of Muhammad.

Bukhari presented one example of Muhammad's response to women: "Allah's Apostle once said to a group of women: 'I have not seen anyone more deficient in intelligence and religion than you. A cautious, sensible man could be led astray by some of you.' The women asked, 'O Allah's Apostle, what is deficient in our intelligence and religion?' He said, 'Is not the evidence of two women equal to the witness of one man?' They replied in the affirmative. He said, 'This is the deficiency of your intelligence....Is it not true that a woman can neither pray nor fast during her menses?' The women replied in the affirmative. He said, 'This is the deficiency in your religion.'"

Bukhari also reveals another deficiency of women taken from Part 1, Hadith No. 28: "Women are ungrateful to their husbands and are ungrateful for the favors and the good (charitable deeds done to them). If you have always been good (benevolent) to one of them and then she sees something in you (not of her liking), she will say, 'I have never received any good from you."

With all of these so-called deficiencies, Muslim men still find uses for their women. Following the example of Muhammad, his successors and others, they marry them, make temporary contracts and divorce them at will. Women have no voice, no will and no rights even to their own bodies.

Marriage

Rafiqul Haqq summarizes the significance of marriage in his book *Women in Islam*. He said, quoting from the book *Al-Fiqh ala al-Mazahib al-arba'a* (Volume 4, Page 488): "The accepted understanding in the different schools of jurisprudence is that what has been contracted in marriage is for the benefit of the man from the woman, not the opposite."

The marriage contract is a sign of ownership of the woman's sexual organs and the rest of her body. Haqq also quotes the followers of Imam Shafi: "The most accepted view is that what has been contracted upon is the woman, that is, the benefit derived from her sexual organ."

This is a far cry from the biblical view of marriage in the Book to the Ephesians 5:25-29: "Husbands, love your wives, just as Christ also loved the church and gave Himself for her, that He might sanctify and cleanse her with the washing of water by the word, that He might present her to Himself a glorious church, not having spot or wrinkle or any such thing, but that she should be holy and without blemish. So husbands ought to love their own wives as their own bodies; he who loves his wife loves himself. For no one ever hated his own flesh, but nourishes and cherishes it, just as the Lord does the church." This is hardly the view of Islamic marriage.

The Islamic View of Marriage

The Quran supports the taking of one wife if the husband cannot be fair to more than one. But a Muslim man may marry up to four wives. "If you fear that you will not act justly towards the orphans, marry such women as seem good to you, two, three, four; but if you fear you will not be equitable, then only one, or what your right hands own; so it is likelier you will not be partial."

Islamic men use impartiality as an excuse for immorality. They, like their prophet, seem to be selective in how they view the Quran to their own advantage.

The story is told of an incident in Muhammad's life. His wife Hafsa left to visit her father in another town. After she left, Muhammad invited Maria the Cop, one of his concubines, but not a legal wife, to sleep with him.

Muhammad took her up to Hafsa's apartment. But his wife forgot something and returned to the apartment to find her husband in bed with the other woman. She left and went outside to cry.

Muhammad followed her, promising not to have intercourse with Maria again. But when he broke his promise, he used a text from the Quran to support his behavior: "O Prophet, why forbids thou what God has made lawful to thee, seeking the good pleasure of thy wives? And God is All-forgiving, All-compassionate."

Temporary and Pleasure Marriages

Muslims believe that not only can a man have four wives, but he can take any woman he desires for a period of time known as a temporary marriage, or a marriage of pleasure. Every lust of man is permissible just as long as he and the woman he desires make an agreement.

If it's OK with you and it's OK with her, then the Quran says, it's OK with Allah. All he has to do is provide her with housing and necessities, and she in turn satisfies all his sexual demands with no exceptions.

Early Marriages

Islam also encourages early marriages. What would be considered illegal in the United States and most countries is not only advocated, but legal in Islamic theocracies.

Muhammad took the 7-year-old daughter of a close friend and married her a year later. When she was offered to him he replied, "She is 8, but dependable!" He was 53 at the time–a difference of 45 years.

In actuality he had picked her out when she was much younger. He would sit her on his lap and play games with her when she was only 5. When she turned 8, Muhammad could no longer wait to have sexual relations with her. So he married her. When he discarded her at the age of 18, he forbade her and his other ex-wives to marry for the rest of their lives.

Muslims believe that a man can take any woman he desires for a period of time known as a temporary marriage, or a marriage of pleasure.

A Muslim tells the story of a young woman, the sister of one of his friends. At the age of 13, when she was developing breasts, her family began to search for someone for her to marry. They were unsuccessful.

An older man came forward and proposed marriage. He was 45, the husband of two other wives and had seven grandchildren. They were married according to the Quran.

On their wedding night she was unprepared for what he required of her. To prove his domination over her, he raped her. She died that same night.

No Place in Paradise

Not only are Muslim women treated with violence and disrespect on earth, they are excluded from Paradise or become the "virgins" that surround each Muslim man's bed.

Muhammad spoke of these virgins when recounting his own trip to the seven heavens. He described the variety of fruits, the rivers of honey, the milk and wine. He saw palaces of crystal, sapphire and diamonds. Within these palaces he saw 70 couches made of gold and emeralds. On them lay virgins, untouched by man and ready for their bridegrooms.

Where did these virgins come from? Are they the wives, sisters and daughters of the men they will now serve for all eternity? Are they female angels? To all of these questions, Muhammad simply replied, "There is no bachelor in Paradise." When asked how he could possibly have sex with 70 virgins he said, "I will be given the strength of a hundred men."

Some Muslims do not agreed with this vision of their prophet. They say women will join their husbands in Paradise. Others who are displeased with their wives will receive other women at their disposal.

How could any woman live with her husband while he partakes of perpetual virgins? Muhammad thought himself to have his pick of women. He told his first wife, Khadija, "Oh Khadija, know that God has wedded me to Mary, Christ's mother in Paradise."

He repeated the same story to his favorite wife, Aiysha. "Oh Aiysha, didn't you know that God Almighty in Heaven wedded me to Mary the daughter of Imran, to Kulthum, Moses' sister and to Assiya, wife of the Pharoah."

The Devaluing of Women

Whether on earth or in Heaven, the women of Islam are fated to remain powerless by the tenets of their own religion. The devaluing of women was learned early in pre-Islamic cultures.

Not just an issue for the afterlife only, female children were often killed and buried. The mothers bore the shame of not only bearing them, but burying them. To a woman in that culture a son was a prize, but a woman was of no value.

Muhammad discontinued this practice and gave women the right to life. But he refused to give them a life of rights. Instead he formed a religion and set an example for the exploitation and violation of women that continues today everywhere his beliefs are espoused.

In the Islamic culture, women are not considered as equals. Their word carries only half as much weight as a man's. They receive less inheritance than their male counterparts. They are not allowed to pray in the mosque along side men.

> God has won the gender war for the women of Islam. He has come to set the captives free and heal the brokenhearted.

Basically, they are not free. They are enslaved beneath layers of clothing and veiled faces. They are discarded in divorce and cast aside for other wives. And they are traded like cattle in marriage and refused the rewards of Paradise.

Islamic women are devalued in every corner of society and every aspect of life. They are doomed forever to be under the foot of the man who dominates them. And at the hands of men who beat and kill them for the sake of their "honor," they face death daily.

Until they escape the clutches of the demonic spirits behind Islam, these women cannot possibility know the freedom, love, acceptance and identity that comes from becoming a child of the living God. But God says to those women still in captivity, chained with oppression and deep bondage: "The Spirit of the Lord is upon Me, Because He has anointed Me To preach the gospel to the poor; He has sent Me to heal the brokenhearted, To proclaim liberty to the captives And recovery of sight to the blind, To set at liberty those who are oppressed; To proclaim the acceptable year of the Lord" (Luke 4:18-19).

God has won the gender war for the women of Islam. He has already gained the victory in the war between men and women. And He's come to set the captives free and heal the brokenhearted.

eleven

Looking for Common Ground
Cross Purposes

To hear some people talk about it the only thing that separates Islam from Christianity is 600 years. Many like Pope John Paul II are calling for a coming together of Muslims and Christians.

On Sunday, November 18, 2001, the Pope announced the Catholic Church's intention to hold an Assisi on January 24, 2002. He said that he was inviting the representatives of the world's religions to come "...to pray for the overcoming of opposition and the promotion of authentic peace. In particular, we wish to bring Christians and Muslims together to proclaim to the world that religion must never be a reason for conflict, hatred and violence. In this historic moment, humanity needs to see gestures of peace and to hear words of hope."

His call like that of many others is an attempt to create an ecumenical atmosphere that results in a "one world" faith.

Maybe he has forgotten the response of the young Turk, Mehmet Ali Agca who shot him on May 13, 1981, while he was riding through

St. Peter's Square in Rome. Even while the Pope was trying to move the Roman Catholic theology toward modern thought, Agca declared in a written letter to the Pope that he shot him because he wanted to kill "the supreme commander of the Crusades."

Back to the Crusades

The war of 1,000 years ago still rages. Even Osama bin Laden and his followers trace the roots of their hatred to the clash between Christianity and Islam in the 11th century during the Crusades. To them being an American is to be a Crusader. To be a Crusader is to be an infidel. And to be an infidel is to be the target for Jihad. A treatise authored in the late 1990s by bin Laden was titled the *Declaration of the World Islamic Front for Jihad Against the Jews and the Crusaders.*

In an article by Bob Davis of the *Star-Telegram* in Forth Worth, Texas, bin Laden describes his mission: "The ruling to kill the Americans and their allies—civilians and military—is an individual duty for

> In looking for the way to reach out to Muslims around the world, we will not find common ground in our beliefs or doctrines.

every Muslim who can do it in any country in which it is possible to do it, in order to liberate the Al Aksa Mosque and the holy mosque from their grip, and in order for their armies to move out of all the lands of Islam, defeated and unable to threaten any Muslim."

The details of the Crusades have not been forgotten by bin Laden and others. They cannot forget that on July 15, 1099, a wave of Crusaders conquered Jerusalem and for two days massacred Muslims and Jews. The streets flowed with blood as the warriors of the cross declared "Deus volt, God wills it."

But God didn't will it. Neither does He support the cry of Muslims "Death to the infidels."

Vengeance belongs to God alone and not to man. Paul in his letter to the Church at Rome declares in Chapter 12, verses 19-20: "Beloved, do not avenge yourselves, but rather give place to wrath; for it is written, 'Vengeance is Mine, I will repay,' says the Lord. Therefore 'If your enemy is hungry, feed him; If he is thirsty, give him a drink; For in so doing you will heap coals of fire on his head.'" The answer to the injustice and hatred of the past, isn't vengeance, but love.

Beyond the Differences

In looking for the way to reach out to Muslims around the world, we will not find common ground in our beliefs or doctrines. Our differences go beyond the gap of 600 years.

That, of course, is not the opinion expressed in *The Idiot's Guide to Understanding Islam.* It says, "Given that both religions began with a charismatic leader, it is not surprising that their relations would be equally charged with emotion, fervor and sometimes conflict. Islam accepts the founder of Christianity, Jesus Christ, as a true prophet from God, while denying that he is a god or God Himself. The Quran even devotes whole passages in commenting on the Christian religion. Christianity, which came before Islam, has not yet accepted the validity of Muhammad's message and consequently Christians know little of this rival faith."

Closing the Gap

Christianity is not a rival of Islam. The way to close the gap between us doesn't lie in an ecumenical approach, a theological discussion or an argument that will drive us further apart.

The first step in bringing Muslims to a saving knowledge of Jesus Christ is warfare—not with flesh and blood, but in the spirit. The Apostle Paul wrote in 2 Corinthians 10:3-5, "For though we walk in the flesh, we do not war according to the flesh. For the weapons of our warfare are not carnal but mighty in God for pulling down strongholds, casting down arguments and every high thing that exalts itself against the knowledge of God, bringing every thought into captivity to the obedience of Christ."

We fight a battle between light and darkness, and truth and deception. The false gospel of Islam holds every Muslim captive to its lies. Jesus has come to expose every hidden thing of darkness and set the captives free.

Binding the Strongman

The first thing every one of us can do is pray for those bound by the strongman of Islam. When we pray that God will bind the strongman and along with him the spirits of fear, sin, self-justification, works, hatred, revenge, death, bloodshed, lying and lust, and release the captives to enjoy the freedom Jesus has purchased, we pave the way for the Holy Spirit to touch the hearts of Muslims.

In Matthew 12:29, Jesus said, "How can one enter a strong man's house and plunder his goods, unless he first binds the strong man? And then he will plunder his house." Before we can take the spoils of battle we have to bind the strongman.

Luke says it this way in Chapter 11, verses 21-22: "When a strong man, fully armed, guards his own palace, his goods are in peace. But when a stronger than he comes

Those held captive to the fear, death and destruction of Islam will continue to be its prisoners as long as Satan is fully armed and standing as the strongman in their lives.

upon him and overcomes him, he takes from him all his armor in which he trusted, and divides his spoils."

It is a mistake to underestimate the enemy. Satan has held those in Islam in bondage by his demonic spirits of fear, lying, divination, whoredom, idolatry, perverseness, jealousy, error and antichrist. And he has used the fear of death as his greatest weapon. Hebrews 2:14-15 says, "Inasmuch then as the children have partaken of flesh and blood, He Himself likewise shared in the same, that through death He might destroy him who had the power of death, that is, the devil, and release those who through fear of death were all their lifetime subject to bondage."

Those held captive to the fear, death and destruction of Islam will continue to be its prisoners as long as Satan is fully armed and standing as the strongman in their lives. A stronger One, Jesus, has come and taken all of Satan's armor and weapons. As believers in Jesus we must take the promise of our Commander in Chief seriously.

Jesus said in Luke 10:19: "Behold, I give you the authority to trample on serpents and scorpions, and over all the power of the enemy, and nothing shall by any means hurt you." He is waiting for us to exercise our authority and power over all the powers of the enemy and do battle for the hearts of Muslims.

Doctrines of Demons

The same deception that holds Muslims today has drawn others. The false light of Islam is the same that revered the writings of other prophets throughout history. It opened the door for other doctrines of demons including Joseph Smith and Mormonism, Charles T. Russell and the Jehovah's Witnesses, Mary Baker Eddy and Christian Science, and Ellen G. White and the Seventh-Day Adventists.

The transcendent experiences of Muhammad are no different than the other voices that birthed the cults of recent years and the leaders that led their followers to death in Guyana, South Africa and Waco, Texas. The false light of Satan and his seducing doctrines of demons has only one destination—death.

There is no middle ground between darkness and light and truth and deception. Let's look at some of the lies that have trapped Muslims.

Jesus—Son of God or Another Prophet

Jesus, Who often throughout His ministry on earth preferred to call Himself "the Son of Man," declared in John 14:6-7, "I am the way, the truth, and the life. No one comes to the Father except through Me. If you had known Me, you would have known My Father also; and from now on you know Him and have seen Him."

Jesus left no question as to Who He was. He also didn't leave any "wiggle room" to get to His Father, Jehovah, Almighty God. He is the appointed way. There are no other paths, roads or ways to God.

But the Quran doesn't share this view of Jesus. "O Mary! God gives you the good news of a word from Him. You will be given a son; his name will be the Messiah, Jesus, the Son of Mary. He will be noble in this world and in the Hereafter. He will be among those who are closest to God" (Sura 3:45-46).

To Muhammad and his followers, Jesus was the "Son of Mary," a "noble" person in the world and Someone Who would be "among the closest to God" in the Hereafter. He was not, in their view, the Son of God and the only way to the Father.

Reading further into the Quran and its many commentaries, Jesus is portrayed as a dutiful and obedient boy Who obeyed His mother. He reached manhood, began His mission as a prophet and became a good Jew. According to the Quran, Jesus had a hard time getting people to listen to Him, didn't attract large crowds and only did a few miracles. His disciples,

> Sin is a nonexistent concept for Muslims, so salvation isn't even an issue.

whose names aren't even mentioned, doubted Him. He encountered fierce opposition and was killed.

After that, nothing else happened.

For them, Jesus is definitely not God. Apparently in their reading of the New Testament they missed the multitudes, the miracles, the resurrection and the Acts of the Apostles who eventually gave their lives for their belief in Jesus Christ.

Original Sin—Does It Really Exist?

Sin is a nonexistent concept for Muslims, so salvation isn't even an issue.

Islam does not believe in original sin. They believe that man is born without sin. In fact, they think Adam and Eve were immediately forgiven of their sin of disobeying God in the Garden of Eden. The tenets of Islam teach that God doesn't need to provide atonement for man's sins because He can already forgive anyone, anytime.

But the Bible has much to say on the subject of sin. It is very specific on how sin separated man and woman from God in the Garden of Eden. It describes how it was passed from bloodline to bloodline and carries with it the punishment of death. It tells how sin in someone's life brings with it sickness, disease and demonic strongholds of every kind.

But most importantly, the Bible says sin is the reason that God sent His Son to earth. Then on a cross, Jesus shed His blood and paid the price for the sins of all mankind—past, present and future. Paul writes in 1 Corinthians 15:3: "...Christ died for our sins according to the Scriptures."

What About the Other Doctrines?

What about all the other things Christian's believe. Can Christians and Muslims find some common ground there?

No, not really. Let's go down the list of differences and see exactly what Muslims believe.

The Trinity – God is not divided into parts. That is a characteristic of the demonic and of idols.

Jesus, the Only Begotten Son – God doesn't have any children, so Jesus couldn't be His Son.

Salvation and Redemption – Works are the only way Muslims get to Heaven, so salvation and redemption are nonexistent concepts in Islam.

Confession of Sin – Even though they don't believe in original sin, sin can happen. If you sin you can ask for forgiveness. You don't need a mediator or facilitator. The Quran and other commentaries mention though that even Muhammad wasn't sure you would receive forgiveness when you asked.

The Holy Spirit – There is no concept of a Holy Spirit in Islam. The closest they come to believing in a divine spirit is the angel Gabriel who they believe was the messenger who brought revelation to Muhammad.

The Word of God – Muslims believe that the Word of God is full of errors and contradictions, and doesn't contain the authentic writings of the prophets. They recognized only the Torah, or first five books of the Old Testament, the Psalms and the four gospels of the New Testament.

The Power of Love

The world will continue to seek a common ground for discussion in the natural. While they do, we must continue to battle for the captives of Islam who have been so greatly deceived. Whatever we do, we must do in the love of God.

Muslims do not know the love of God. They fearfully serve a harsh, impersonal, idolatrous deity who has no real use for them. He uses them like they use others. The path of Allah is filled with blood, but not blood

> **Muslims must know that the true God of Abraham, Isaac and Jacob is not angry with them, but loves them with a father's love. He is their "Abba, Father."**

that can cleanse, save and transform lives together.

When we reach out to Muslims we must go without fear. First John 4:18 says, "Perfect love casts out fear." We cannot battle for their freedom when we are captives to fear ourselves.

Love breaks down barriers and removes the hardness of a person's heart. Jesus loves every Muslim. So we must do the same.

We must remember that for Muslims to reject Allah is to face his wrath and the judgment of Hell. Any Muslim who converts to Christianity pays a price most of us in Western culture cannot conceive of paying. They face losing everything and everyone they love—and sometimes even their lives.

Reza F. Safa in his book *Inside Islam* shares some of his own story after his conversion: "I was not instantly free from the fear of Islam.

One night shortly after my conversion I had an encounter with the spirit of fear in my room. I woke up from a nightmare in the middle of the night, but as I opened my eyes, it seemed as though some awful sort of being who was full of darkness was standing over my head.

"Suddenly, I felt something heavy and dreadful land on my chest. I realized that I was not dreaming, but that I was confronting demonic forces. I knew the only way to defeat those beings was to rebuke them and call upon the name of Jesus."

Reza did just that and has never feared Islam again. His testimony is a chilling account of the strength of the grip that holds Muslims within the power of Satan's control.

Message of Freedom

Muslims need to know that they can be free. They must no longer be captives to fear. They must know and experience for themselves the transforming, life-changing love of God. They must know that the true God of Abraham, Isaac and Jacob is not angry with them, but loves them with a father's love. He is their "Abba, Father."

Romans 8:15 says, "For you did not receive the spirit of bondage again to fear, but you received the Spirit of adoption by whom we cry out, 'Abba, Father.'" What a comfort this is for every Muslim who gives their heart and life to Jesus.

This message of freedom from captivity and fear is ours to share with Muslims everywhere. We as the Church of Jesus Christ have been given His same commission. We must go as He did, and know that we are anointed to set the captives free—even those trapped in Islam.

This is our message of freedom. It is the same message Jesus declared.

The Spirit of the Lord is upon Me, Because He has anointed Me To preach the gospel to the poor; He has sent Me to heal the brokenhearted, To proclaim liberty to the captives And recovery of sight to the blind, To set at liberty those who are oppressed; To proclaim the acceptable year of the Lord (Luke 4:18-19).

We must preach this message of peace and freedom *without compromise.* If we draw back and do not move forward with the boldness and confidence that is ours in Jesus Christ, we water down His message and remove its power to change lives.

Some say, "You can't just come out a tell a Muslim that Jesus is the Son of God and the only way to Heaven!"

Others add, "Do what Paul teaches and be all things to all men."

Our opinions have no power to change lives, only the Word of God and the truth within it goes into the hearts of men and women and returns bearing the fruit of salvation. God's Word alone goes forth and does not return void without accomplishing its purpose and intended result.

> Jesus preached the truth without compromise. And we must let everyone know the truth that has the power to set them free.

Jesus is not *a* lord, He is *the* Lord, God Almighty. He is not one of many ways, but "the Way, the Truth and the Life." I'm sure that in Jesus' day, many would have cautioned Him to pull back from the harshness of His message. After all "you don't want to scare anyone off."

But Jesus preached the truth without compromise. And He expects the same of us. We must let everyone know the truth that has the power to set them free.

Therefore if the Son makes you free, you shall be free indeed (John 8:36).

twelve

Breaking Down the Barriers
Message of the Heart

The story is being duplicated all across the United States and around the world. This particular pilgrimage began for an upstate New Yorker while he was serving during the Gulf War in 1991. He later was transferred to Pakistan where he saw something that impressed him.

He told a reporter for the *Dallas Morning News* that it was the piety of the people. The special edition of the Religion Section of the newspaper chronicled not just one story of conversion to Islam, but four.

Abdal Malik Rezeski of Dallas had a Jewish father and Christian mother. Yet he chose neither religion for himself.

Why you might be asking? He said it was the first religion that made sense to him.

Each of the other three converts said it was the challenge and discipline that attracted them to Islam. Maybe none of them had considered how hard it is to be a Christian. Or worse, maybe they had never seen a Christian they wanted to be like. Possibly none of them had seen Jesus in the life of anyone around them.

Without Debate

A Muslim sees a Christian and braces for an argument. When they see most of us, they must think, *Here comes the Bible-thumper who wants to debate my doctrine and tell me just how wrong I am.*

I wouldn't blame them if they walked the other way. No one likes to be attacked for any reason. But Muslim converts are rising. Maybe like the young man from Dallas, or the other three converts, they have never really heard Jesus' message or known about His love for them.

In Reza F. Safa's book *Inside Islam*, he tells the story of one newly converted Muslim. After receiving Jesus as His Lord and Savior, he was zealous about evangelizing other Muslims. So one evening he joined Reza and some other believers on the streets of Stockholm, Sweden.

As Reza talked with another man, he couldn't help but hear yelling. "I'll kill you! I'll kill you!" The new Iranian believer was arguing with a Muslim from Pakistan.

He walked over and asked the new convert what he had said to anger the Muslim man so much. He said, "I just told him the truth: Muhammad is dead, and Jesus is alive."

The young man learned quickly that his truthful yet brash approach pushed the Muslim man away. He watched as Reza talked calmly with the man from Pakistan. He told him lovingly about Jesus. He watched as Reza tried not to win points, but to win his heart.

An Open Door

Love is the thing that can effectively provide an open door and break down the barriers that stand between Muslims and Christians. We need to prayerfully, with the help of the Holy Spirit, share the gospel with every Muslim. We must share the message of Jesus the same way He did—with all the love in the world.

Christians need to get in touch with the heart of Jesus. He had no problem removing the barriers and the obstacles of a person's heart. He did it with the religious—Nicodemus and Zacchaeus. He did it with the lunatic—the mad man of Gederah. He did it with the sinful—Mary Magdalene and the woman at the well.

Everywhere Jesus went he took the love of God with Him. His compassion and love opened the door for lives to be changed by His truth.

Sharing the Truth

So how do you share the truth of the gospel with a Muslim?

The first thing is to remember that the heart and needs of men and women are the same all over the world. Regardless of their race, religion, gender or circumstances, people are still looking for love and meaning in life. Whether they are Muslims, Hindus, atheists, Mormons, Jews or simply secular humanists, they all are effected by sin, sickness, fear, pain and death.

> **Love is the thing that can effectively provide an open door and break down the barriers that stand between Muslims and Christians.**

Everyone needs something. Some need healing. Others acceptance. Still others forgiveness and love. We must remember that the gospel is for all. Paul said it this way in Romans 1:16: "I am not ashamed of the gospel of Christ, for it is the power of God to salvation for everyone who believes, for the Jew first and also for the Greek."

There is no limit to the power of God to change lives. But first people must hear. And they can only hear if we go and tell them. Romans 10:17 says, "Faith comes by hearing, and hearing by the word of God."

As believers who have already experienced the life-changing power and love of God in our own lives, we need to take the message that turned our lives around to others. We need to help open the prison doors and let the captives out.

Isaiah 42:6-7 says, "I, the Lord, have called You in righteousness, And will hold Your hand; I will keep You and give You as a covenant to the people, As a light to the Gentiles, To open blind eyes, To bring out prisoners from the prison, Those who sit in darkness from the prison house."

Jesus is the One Who has purchased freedom for all. Now it's our privilege to take that message of freedom to the prisoners, take the key of our authority and set the captives free. It can be done. Nothing is too hard for God.

Accepting the Mission

Exercise your privilege and take on the mission that Jesus has commissioned you to do—GO. You can share the love and good news of Jesus Christ. But as you go to share the gospel, remember these things:

➤ Never forget the open door that friendship brings. When we offer friendship to a Muslim, we are providing God an open door to their heart. Everyone needs a friend. Do not underestimate what God can do through the everyday presence of a Christian friend in the life of a Muslim.

➤ Share the gospel with love. Love is the barrier breaker.

➤ Know that the Holy Spirit will prepare someone's heart and help you as you share your testimony and the Word of God.

➤ Show them what the Word of God has to say about God, His love, salvation, forgiveness and how they can know God through a personal relationship with Jesus Christ.

➤ Remember, it's not your job to bring conviction. Love them and let the Holy Spirit touch their heart. You plant the seed and let God bring the harvest.

➤ Pray that God will confirm His Word with signs and wonders. Miracles and signs are for the unbeliever. Believe God for His power to perform great signs, wonders, miracles and acts of His Spirit.

➤ Pray that God will also speak to every Muslim through supernatural dreams and visions. What God did for Saul, he can do for the Muslim man and woman you are praying for and sharing Jesus with. He can seal their instruction while they are sleeping.

The Love of God

Also keep in mind that some Muslims don't like to discuss social or religious topics with Christians and consider doing so to bring defilement. If you have a friend who feels this way, your love of Jesus will speak volumes without you ever saying a word to them.

If you know a Muslim who has a positive attitude regarding Christianity, but who isn't comfortable talking with you about the Bible, talk instead about social issues that might lead into a conversation about religion. If the Muslims you are acquainted with would rather attack your beliefs than talk, answer their questions with a question. You might be surprised how effective that technique will be and where the discussion might lead.

Be sure to take advantage of every opportunity to answer their questions in a way that will direct them to the truth. When you do have an opportunity to share the message of the gospel, remember to keep it simple.

Do not underestimate the power of God's love. Open your heart to these words by Reza F. Safa, a former Shiite Muslim: "There is no greater experience for a Muslim than tasting the agape love of God. To know God as a loving and caring Father is a foreign concept to a Muslim.

"Muslims have never felt nor experienced the love of God in a personal way. Muslims know God as an awesome, all-powerful deity who cannot be approached by men. They fear Him and His wrath."

Safa said it was the love of Christians that changed his life: "It was this love shown to me by the Christians who gave me the gospel that drew me to Jesus. It was pure, holy and without any deception or flaws.

"I was always greatly loved by my family and friends. But the love that I experienced from those believers was totally different. It was unlike any other love I'd ever known in my life. It convicted me. It made me see the real me. It was like a spotlight shining deep into my being."

Remember for a moment how you felt the first time you really received and felt the unconditional love of God in your life. Man's love is conditional and changeable. But God's love never changes.

I will never forget the day I experienced the love of the Father. It transformed me. I know it also changed you forever.

Most of us have heard John 3:16 all of our lives, but the day we experienced it for ourselves is unforgettable. "For God so loved the world that He gave His only begotten Son, that whoever believes in Him should not perish but have everlasting life." Imagine once again how it felt to experience that for the first time.

That's the way a Muslim feels when they hear that God is no longer angry with them. That's what goes through their heart when they can breathe a sigh of relief and know that Allah's wrath will not send them to a place of eternal punishment. That's what hits every cell and nerve of their body when they can believe for the first time ever that they don't have to work their way to a God Who will only push them away.

> God's arms of love are opened wide to all who come to Him with a heart open to receive and believe. Only Jesus can do what man cannot.

What a freeing thought!

God's arms of love are opened wide to *all* who come to Him with a heart open to receive and believe. Only Jesus can do what man cannot. Romans 5:8 says, "God demonstrates His own love toward us, in that while we were still sinners, Christ died for us."

When we walked away from Him, He waited patiently for us to return. When we shook our fist in His face and cursed Him, He loved us. When our sin took us places we didn't want to go and kept us longer than we wanted to stay, He died for us so that we could be forever free.

What a love God has for all of us! It's hard to resist such love.

That is why when Muslims receive God's love, they are willing to do anything and everything for Him. They are willing to sacrifice everything. They have tasted God's love and goodness through Jesus and they will never be the same again.

A Heart Encounter

The day Muslims hear of God's love for them they will think long and hard about the 18-hour pilgrimages they have made to the tomb of a dead man. They will remember the fear, the pain and the endless works to reach a god who wanted nothing to do with them. They will feel the emptiness and know that they have to know this God Whose love reaches deep into their heart.

The most important thing you can share with Muslims is the love of God you have experienced for yourself. If you can love them, you can win them and God can save them. Love does conquer all—if it's the love of God.

> ...Christ may dwell in your hearts through faith; that you, being rooted and grounded in love, may be able to comprehend with all the saints what is the width and length and depth and height—to know the love of Christ which passes knowledge; that you may be filled with all the fullness of God (Ephesians 3:17-19).

about the author

Dr. Henry Malone, co-founder of Vision Life Ministries, is sounding the battle cry for freedom everywhere. Formerly a senior pastor of 28 years, with 41 years of combined ministry background, Henry is bringing the message of deliverance and inner healing to churches, ministries, pastors, families and individuals, and has worked extensively in the Muslim world since 1976.

Since 1989, his commitment to bring freedom to the captives and healing to the brokenhearted has sent him to cities all across the United States and around the world proclaiming and demonstrating the works of the kingdom of God. Henry presents Freedom and Fullness Seminars and releases the ministry of Jesus in groups and one on one to bring healing, deliverance and freedom.

Since 1992, Henry has trained, equipped and released interns for ministry in the areas of deliverance and emotional healing. In 1998, he established the School of Deliverance Ministry to help local churches bring victory to those experiencing the bondage of demonic oppression and the pain of emotional trauma. Each year, Henry also helps train pastors in third-world nations and travels to churches and conferences speaking on behalf of world missions.

Henry and his wife, Tina, have two grown children, three grandchildren and live in Grand Prairie, Texas. He also serves as an elder of Shady Grove Church in Grand Prairie, Texas.

Freedom and Fullness Seminars

This two-day seminar is an in-depth look at the 2-5-14 strategy introduced in Dr. Henry Malone's book *Shadow Boxing*. Specifically designed to lead a church or group through corporate deliverance, the seminar begins on Friday night and continues through late Saturday afternoon. The seminar includes both intensive teaching and ministry time, and includes an extensive workbook. A teaching and ministry team that has been trained or is in the process of being trained by Vision Life Ministries leads each seminar.

The seminar teaching includes the following topics:

➤ The War of the Ages
➤ Proclaiming Liberty
➤ Two Ways Satan Gains Ground: Intrusion and Legal Ground
➤ The Five Doors: Disobedience, Inner Vows, Curses, Emotional Trauma, Unforgiveness
➤ Strongholds and Root Spirits
➤ How to Break Curses and Tear Down Strongholds
➤ How to Walk in Freedom

For churches interested in more information regarding this exciting and life-changing seminar, please contact:

Vision Life Ministries
P.O. Box 153691
Irving, TX 75015
972-251-7170
www.visionlife.org

The School of Deliverance Ministry

The School of Deliverance Ministry offers approximately 40 hours of training and is designed to encourage, train and equip those whose gifting and desire is to demonstrate and extend the kingdom of God through deliverance and inner healing. The School of Deliverance Ministry is a foundational course that will benefit and strengthen any believer.

The curriculum includes such topics as:

- The Fourteen Root Spirits
- The Authority of the Believer
- The Authority and Faith Connection
- The Yoke-Destroying Anointing
- The Preparation of the Warrior
- Developing a Listening Ear
- Discerning of Spirits
- The Emotional Healing of the Brokenhearted

The actual dynamics of deliverance are also modeled, demonstrated and incorporated in many exercises throughout the course. The school may be taken in a regular or intensive format. For churches interested in hosting a school or individuals interested in attending, please contact:

Vision Life Ministries
P.O. Box 153691
Irving, TX 75015
972-251-7170
www.visionlife.org

Deliverance Ministry Internship

The Deliverance Ministry Internship is specifically designed for those with a calling, gifting and passion for setting the captives free and healing the brokenhearted. Part One of the internship provides intensive small group and one-on-one training to enable each person to become more effective in leading personal ministry sessions. Part Two involves a personal mentoring and discipleship for a six month period.

Both Parts One and Two of the internship are built on the foundation established during the School of Deliverance Ministry. Interns receive a minimum of 60 hours of training in a limited group setting during Part One, and six months in Part Two. All prospective interns must have both pastoral approval and a recommendation to participate and must make application to the program to be accepted.

For more information, please contact:

Vision Life Ministries
P.O. Box 153691
Irving, TX 75015
972-251-7170
www.visionlife.org

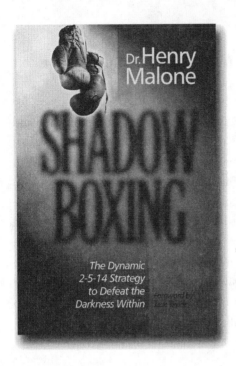

Take Back Spiritual Ground

Also available
by Dr. Malone

Portals—they exist all around the earth and open a door to the presence of God or to the demonic. Step into the realm of the supernatural with *Portals to Cleansing*. Discover how spiritual ground is taken and how it is released. Learn the keys to reclaiming your land, home, possessions and animals from the power of Satan and his demonic forces. Experience the peace that comes from the cleansing of all you possess. Walk into a portal of God's presence that will take you deeper into the realm of the Spirit and change your life forever.

A Portals to Cleansing kit is also available. This unique kit contains wooden stakes with scriptures, anointing oil and instruction booklet to help you reclaim your land and property.

ORDER TODAY!

Paperback–$12

Portals to Cleansing Kit–$12

Vision Life Publications
PO Box 153691 • Irving, Texas 75015
972-251-7170 • www.visionlife.org

Order Form

You may place an order for product using any of the following:

- ➤ Call to place your order: **(972) 251-7170**
- ➤ Fax your order: **(972) 254-1510**
- ➤ Postal orders: **Vision Life Ministries, P.O. Box 153691, Irving, TX 75015**
- ➤ Order online: **www.visionlife.org**

Title	Price		Quantity		Amount
Islam Unmasked	$10	x	_____	=	_____
Portals to Cleansing	$12	x	_____	=	_____
Portals to Cleansing Kit	$12	x	_____	=	_____
Shadow Boxing	$12	x	_____	=	_____

Shipping and Handling _____
(Please add $5 for the first book and $2 for each additional book)

Total _____

____ Please send more information about Freedom and Fullness seminars

____ Please send more information about The School of Deliverance Ministry

____ Please send more information about Deliverance Ministry Internship

_____

Name (Please print clearly)

_____

Address   Apt.

_____

City   State   ZIP

_____

Country   Phone

_____

E-Mail

Method of Payment

____ Check/Money Order (Payable to Vision Life Ministries)   ____VISA   ____MasterCard

_____

Card Number   Expiration Date

_____

Card Holder (Please print clearly)

_____

Signature